WINDSOR SPARES

The Prince Harry & Prince Andrew Soap Opera

NIGEL CAWTHORNE

GIBSON SQUARE

This edition first published by Gibson Square

gibsonsquare.com
rights@gibsonsquare.com

CONTENTS

Spare and Sparer

When Prince Harry published his controversial, confessional *Spare* with too much information in January 2023, he pushed another 'spare' out of the headlines. Prince Andrew has yet to favour us with his misery memoirs, but perhaps Harry's doorstopper provides a useful insight into his uncle who is now even more spare than Harry. Harry is fifth in the line of succession, while Andrew is eighth. At birth, both started in the third place, so things are not going well for them career-wise.

Clearly, Andrew is arrogant enough to have coveted the top job, while in his autobiography his nephew seems to make public his brush with ambition. The women he met while a bachelor, he said, suffered from 'throne syndrome'. They would be 'visibly fitting herself for the crown the moment she shook my hand'. It is only the monarch and his consort who get to sit on the throne and wear a crown, so the girlfriends had already factored in various subsequent steps that needed to happen first. Princesses only get to wear those royal hats that look like dinner plates worn at an angle. It clearly unsettled Harry to be desirable for something he would never have.

Andrew never had such problems. He was Prince Philip and the Queen's favourite. Yet, Harry saw himself as a 'very unbrilliant boy' and suffered what he saw as being treated like a 'nullity'. Andrew on the other hand was always groomed for a role in the palace that didn't exist. Unlike Harry, whose future was secure due to the millions he would one day inherit from his mother, Andrew would inherit very little because Philip had very little if anything to pass on to his children. His parents needed the Firm to provide for Andrew and, being treated like anything but a nullity, he came to believe unshakeably in his own monumental importance to the monarchy in Britain.

Harry also compares himself to Hamlet in his memoir: 'Lonely prince, obsessed with a dead parent, watches remaining parent fall in love with dead parents' usurper'. Hamlet had been robbed of the throne by his uncle who murdered his father and married his mother. Hamlet plots, ineptly, to avenge his father's murder an act which would have, presumably, put him on the throne, if only he hadn't screwed up first. Harry's uncle Andrew is not motivated enough to go through all these shenanigans. But still, like Hamlet, Harry struggles forever with his emotions.

At least, Harry writes, 'maybe I'm a foundling? Because I am a nervous wreck.' He has just told a courtier that there is no photograph of him using cocaine in order not to spoil the Queen's fiftieth jubilee with bad headlines. It was a gamble that paid off for Harry. Though not for his nerves evidently.

Despite drawing the parallel with Hamlet, Harry was not a natural fan of Shakespeare's play. 'I slammed the books shut,' he says. 'No, thank you.' It didn't help that his father couldn't stop quoting Shakespeare at every turn, if he wasn't regaling his sons with ancestral facts. Another big turn off.

But the Bard would not leave him alone. At Eton, he was forced to play the drunkard Conrade in *Much Ado About Nothing*—a bit of typecasting, he thought. His father came to watch the production and laughed at all the wrong moments. Quizzed afterwards by his perplexed son, Charles admitted that Prince Philip did exactly the same when he came to watch him perform. Was it a subtle case of royal heckling? His interest in Shakespeare, however, is piqued after his great-grandmother, the Queen Mother, dies. He regrets not asking her more about her distant ancestors in Glamis, home to Macbeth who murdered the king to take the throne. Hmm.

There is no indication that Prince Andrew has ever had more than a passing acquaintance with the works of Shakespeare. Although the Queen taught him to read herself, neither she nor Prince Philip were particularly interested in the inside of the many libraries she owned. However, Andrew was a friend of actor Kevin Spacey's, organising a private, after-hours tour of Buckingham Palace for him and Ghislaine Maxwell in 2002. They were photographed sitting on the thrones used in the Queen's 1953 coronation. Shortly after Spacey became artistic director of the Old Vic where he played the title role in Shakespeare's *Richard III,* a king who seized the throne after murdering his older brother and the two princes in the Tower. If Andrew had done that at the time—killing Charles and the then unwed William and Harry—he would now be king. Spacey's royal role received plaudits on both sides of the Atlantic. It didn't help him either, as both he and Andrew are today struggling with severe image failures.

Harry feigned to have no interest in history, particularly family history. But he also said he wished he'd asked his great grandmother, the Queen Mother, more about her husband George VI, who was a second son who took the crown after his older brother Edward VIII abdicated to marry

American divorcee Wallis Simpson. That must have felt a bit too close to home. He left it a bit late in any case, she was 101.

One thing Harry does observe in *Spare*, as he violates the omerta of the royal family that you do not air dirty laundry in public, is his response to the memoir by his mother's butler Paul Burell. Unlike his, the money wasn't going to charity. 'It was merely one man's self-justifying, self-centring version of events', he writes. Without irony he adds, 'It made my blood boil'. One can almost hear the vigour with which Charles and William nodded at reading this passage. Harry seems to have redefined his job as spare to become the Firm's professional Embarrassment-in-Chief and found far better professional support than his uncle to do so. Or maybe he is modest enough to listen to them, or, at any rate, let professionals write his autobiography for him for maximum effect.

Number Twos

You don't have to take too much interest in the history of the Royal Family to know that a surprising number of spares have sat on the throne and this may be one reason why they are such enduring headache for the reigning monarch. The odds are considerable and the court can't ignore a spare once the heir is an adult. What if through fate's unknown unknowns, the spare reaches the finish line after all and ends up on the throne? Spares hang around visibly enough, just in case—at least until the heir's own heir and spare are also adults.

The current royal family claims lineage spanning a thousand years beginning with William the Conqueror and the Norman invasion. William was succeeded by his son William Rufus, who died when shot through the chest with an arrow in the New Forest. He was succeeded by his younger brother Henry I who happened to be with the hunting party that day. Historian John Gillingham concluded that Henry's actions 'seem to be pre-meditated: wholly disregarding his dead brother, he rode straight for Winchester, seized the treasury (always the first act of a usurping king), and the next day had himself elected'. It was a good start to the dynasty for his ambitious younger brother.

Any British royal spare can take some heart that the odds in their favour are pretty good if the past is a guide to the future. Richard the Lionheart was succeeded by his brother, John, who had already sought to usurp the throne while Richard was away at the crusades. In 1399, Richard II was dethroned by his cousin Henry VI, leading to the War of the Roses, which resulted in the fratricidal Richard III taking the throne in 1483. He was usurped to two years later by distant cousin Henry VII at the Battle of Bosworth, establishing the Tudor dynasty. Henry VIII took the throne after his older brother Arthur had died, as well as his brother's widow. The list goes on. Charles I succeeded in 1649 after his older brother had died of typhoid at the age of eighteen. Then, after the minor unpleasantness of the Civil War and a short-lived republic, his son Charles II was installed as king. He died without any legitimate heirs, so his younger brother James took over in 1685.

To be sure, sisters joined in the fun too. So there is even hope for Princess Charlotte, the spare in waiting. There was no love lost between Henry's daughters Mary I and Elizabeth I before Elizabeth succeeded her sister in 1558. Elizabeth ordered the execution of her cousin Mary, Queen of Scots, who also had claims on the throne, which then passed to her son James I of England, James VI of Scotland, in 1603. After the Glorious Revolution put Queen Mary and King William on the throne, Anne became queen in 1702, following her sister's death, although her half-brother was her father's legitimate heir. He was, however, barred from the throne on the grounds that he was a Catholic.

It gets even more encouraging for royal spares in more recent history. When Queen Anne died, the rules of primogeniture were again ignored. James's claim to the throne was overridden in favour of a distant cousin, the Elector of Hanover, a German who became George I of England and lived mainly on the continent. Under the Georgians, another steal by a younger brother followed. The dissolute George IV was succeeded by his younger brother William IV, who outraged London by returning from Jamaica with a black mistress and had ten illegitimate children with actress Mrs Jordan.

Queen Victoria wanted to end the litany of royal scandals and aimed to establish her nine royal children as a model family in contrast to her libidinous Hannoverian uncles—though it could be argued that her promiscuous son Bertie was the prince of fun of his day. Bertie was twice cited in the divorce courts before he acceded as Edward VII. His last mistress was Alice Keppel, the great grandmother of Camilla Parker Bowles, now Queen Consort.

Edward VII's spare succeeded as George V due to the convenient demise of the eldest heir, Prince Eddy. Eddy was arguably a prince of fun like his father as he was implicated in a sex scandal—in his case one involving a male brothel. To some historians, he is even put forward posthumously as a possible candidate for Jack the Ripper.

Then, in 1936, we get Edward VIII who fell in love with a scandalous woman (she was twice-married) and in order to marry her had to abdicate in favour of his younger brother George VI. He not only had a stutter and helped win World War Two, but was also Andrew's grandfather and Harry's great-grandfather. If he hadn't become king, all the column inches about the two private lives of the two princes would never have happened (a sobering thought).

So the Windsors have form. Sibling rivalry, if not outright fratricide, is in their DNA. If the accident of birth had initially robbed them of the top job, there was always the possibility that a pandemic, a freak accident or an audacious assassination, or a good old scandal, might thrust them onto the throne.

The old, old rivalry of the heir and the spare goes on as Harry points out. He was never happier than when, at Sandhurst, Crown Prince William had to salute him. William went to university first and only joined the Army after his younger brother, so, for one short per, Harry outranked him.

But at home, the whole family made no bones about it that he was 'the shadow, the support, the Plan B' from as early as he could remember.

'I was brought into the world in case something happened to Willy,' he wrote. 'I was summoned to provide back-up, distraction, diversion and, if necessary, a spare part. Kidney, perhaps. Blood transfusion. Speck of bone marrow. This was all made explicitly clear to me from the start of life's journey and regularly reinforced thereafter.'

There was only one thing for it. Go to America and become the 'king over the water' like his Stuart forebear in the 18th century. Harry had learnt about the ambitions of the Scottish 'Bonnie Prince Charlie' from Mr Hughes-Games, his history master at Eton.

Besides, Meghan is said by some to be lining herself up to be the first woman president. In the US, he could at least be 'First Gentleman'. Hollywood actor Ronald Reagan had made it to the White House. There was no reason that the Suits star of the Netflix generation could not follow in his footsteps helped with a little Windsor fairy dust. If Megan did become President, it would mean a temporary restoration of Britain's rule over the US since his forefather George III lost the American colonies.

Meanwhile Andrew, the older spare, is not doing so well riding shotgun. His prospects as Fergie's Prince charming have long gone up in a cloud of smoke. Now that he's divorced from her, he cannot even look forward to being number two at Weight Watchers or any of her other ventures, from confessional star on Oprah (who would want to hear Andrew's confessions?) to coming up with ideas for royal documentaries or writing children's books. As that bearded sage Karl Marx warned us: 'History repeats itself, first as tragedy, second as farce.'

Spare 2.0

While Harry's discontent with being the spare led according to him to royal fisticuffs with his elder brother—felling a princely necklace and a royal dog bowl in the process—did Andrew feel the same discontent? He certainly had a lifelong rivalry with his brother, now Charles III. Andrew was his mother's favourite, and naturally there was competition for her love from his envious older brother. Andrew was handsome as a teenager, Charles just had big ears. We know that Andrew's greeting ritual of his mother was to bow and then give her two pecks on the cheek. Charles was apparently never allowed such a personal display of affection, Harry tells us. Even at the age of five, the Queen's firm handshake was all he got after she returned from being away for months on end. The only one who ever got close to a hug was Diana

Charles hated their boarding school Gordonstoun and always wanted to go to debonair Eton. His parents wanted him to toughen up, however, which meant horrendous bullying. Gordonstoun's ethos was against 'creative types, sensitive types, bookish types—in other words Pa', who confided in Harry, 'I nearly didn't survive'. Charles's only friend was his teddy bear, which still went with him everywhere as an adult. But Andrew flourished at their school in remote Scotland. While Spartan, it was as posh as Marie Antoinette's play farm where she could pretend to be a peasant. Harry would probably have, too. Like Uncle Matthew, he seems to have read one book (*Of Mice and Men*, short), liked it but didn't think it necessary to read more. Unlike his father, he confides that his pain threshold and disregard for physical safety so high that he becomes scary on a pitch. At Eton, however, there weren't enough bullies for him and his 'red mist' to conquer.

Charles's naval career was undistinguished; Andrew returned from the Falklands a hero. As a bachelor, Charles sowed his wild oats tamely among the county set; Andrew, however, dated models and actresses and any girl in between. Though he missed out, Andrew always fancied Diana, while

Charles told Diana he wished she could be more like Fergie.

When Charles's popularity hit rock bottom after the break-up of his marriage and his continuing association with Camilla Parker-Bowles, he began to suspect that brothers Andrew and Edward were plotting against him. 'Andrew wanted to be me,' a disconsolate Charles told his private secretary Mark Bolland. After Diana said in an interview on *Panorama* that she did not think Charles would be king, he convinced himself that Diana and Fergie had plans to replace him as heir and announce that, in the event of the Queen's death or abdication, Andrew would be regent until William was eighteen. History was studded with regents who went on to become king. Even Britain had one in George IV, formerly the thoroughly disreputable Prince Regent.

Charles fought back, trying to remove Andrew's daughters Beatrice and Eugenie from the royal payroll. But Andrew made efforts to keep his daughters close to the Queen to ensure their future as fully paid-up members of the family. He also wanted Beatrice and Eugenie to retain the rank of working royals and to have round-the-clock security costing £250,000 a year each. They were the only two 'blood princesses' of their generation he argued.

Charles then saw to it that Andrew and Edward were later excluded from a formal lunch celebrating the Queen's Diamond Jubilee. Nor were they seen on the balcony of Buckingham Palace afterwards. Andrew saw this as a demotion. For him, worse was to come.

Following his subsequent disgrace as a result of featuring in the Epstein/Maxwell/Giuffre sex trafficking scandal, there would be no comfortable exile in America for Andrew. Wanted by the FBI as a 'person of interest' he risked being arrested as soon as he set foot on American soil and the US sent a request under the Mutual Legal Assistance Treaty to the Home Secretary to have Andrew interviewed by Scotland Yard. Not even Megan Markle as President would save him. As a woke Hollywood veteran she would recall the fate of Andrew's friend invited to his daughter's 18th birthday, Harvey Weinstein. Andrew never made an endearing impression on her. When she had first meet Andrew, she apparently took him to be the Queen's assistant, or, in Buckingham Palace rather than Tinsel Town lingo, the footman assigned to holding her handbag.

Mummy Boys

Andrew and Harry's lives have certain parallels. Both were born to palace life: Andrew in Buckingham Palace and Harry in Kensington Palace. Clearly, they were going to turn out weird. If, from the time you can first walk and talk, doors are opened for you and flunkeys are always bowing and scraping and calling you 'Your Royal Highness', you are going to get a very skewed view of the world and your own self importance. And both were, of course, mummy's boys.

Harry admits as much. Throughout his *Spare*, he calls Diana 'Mummy'. At the time of writing, he was thirty-eight. About time, he should have got over it.

Was Andrew any different? He himself no doubt thought he was a bit of a swashbuckler when, at the age of twenty, he was stationed at the aircraft carrier HMS *Hermes*. But a senior officer of his observed: 'He's a bit of a mummy's boy. You could never say that about Charles.'

When Charles was born his mother was already undertaking royal duties and tours for her ailing father. He was just four when she became Queen and was occupied full time with her new role and had little time for him as she left him in charge of a fleet of nannies with their own footmen. By the time Andrew came along eight years later, she knew the ropes well enough to take time off to mollycoddle her new infant.

Andrew was to be indulged. She wrote to her cousin, 'the baby is adorable. All in all, he's going to be terribly spoilt by all of us, I'm sure.' Andrew's nanny called him 'Baby Grumpling' for his temper tantrums, Prince Philip called him 'The Boss' as he was wilful and self-possessed. Appearing at a film premiere with a black eye, Philip said that 'The Boss' had done it. Everyone thought he meant the Queen.

The baby prince was named Andrew after his grandfather, Prince Andrew (of Greece and Denmark), who was twice exiled from his native land. He did not set a good example to live up to. Estranged from his wife and son, and his daughters who all married Nazis, he died in Monte Carlo where he had been living on board his mistress's yacht.

Andrew was rarely punished and played practical jokes on the staff, hiding the knives and forks when a footman was laying the table and tying a sentry's shoelaces together. He took a radio apart to bits, tobogganed down the stairs in the Palace on a tea tray, and broke the greenhouse windows with a football. He pranked the Queen Mother with a whoopee cushion, sprinkled itching powder in his mother's bed and climbed onto the roof of Buckingham Palace to turn the TV aerial so that there was no picture when his mother the Queen sat down to watch one of her favourite shows, the Sandown Park horse races. The Queen thought her second son was hilarious.

Rather than being taught by private tutors in the Palace as previous generations of royals had been, Andrew attended a prep school in an attempt to give him a less royal and a somewhat more ordinary childhood. But this had been decided well before his birth. His education followed in the footsteps of Prince Charles, so everything he did Charles had done first and usually better. At the age of eight, he was sent to Heatherdown School in Ascot, not far from Windsor. This earned him the sobriquet 'Action Man Two', which he resented.

Princess Diana wanted her children to be brought up like commoners, too. Andrew had been born in the Belgian Suite of Buckingham Palace, but Harry had first seen the light of day in the Lindo Ward of St Mary's Hospital, Paddington, where William had also been born. Soon after he had to be displayed to the waiting crowds and cameramen on the hospital steps. Starting with Harry, this became the new tradition.

The Queen wasn't totally committed to making Andrew a commoner. He was taught driving by former Formula One world champion Graham Hill, after being given a mini Aston Martin model of the car driven by James Bond in Goldfinger. The Bishop of Norwich took him to a football match of Chelsea vs Norwich, he was showed round Scotland Yard with an Iranian prince, and security officers taught him how to handle a gun. As a youth Andrew was also taught ballroom dancing which ill-prepared him for the disco floor at Tramp. He remained bathed in privilege. He and his younger brother Edward were taken to Lords to be taught how to play cricket and to Wimbledon for tennis coaching, while their boy scouts units were taken to them rather than the other way around. His feeling of being above everyone else showed early on in lots of little ways. Sharing a dormitory with six others, he complained that he was not allowed to watch the TV programmes he watched at home.

Was Diana going to do a better job with young Harry?

Lucky Harry

Harry was nine days premature, and Diana had to be rushed from Windsor Castle to the Lindo Ward of St Mary's at 6.30 that morning. The journey to the hospital was tinged with farce. The unmarked police car escorting the royal couple's Ford Granada was challenged to a race by a young man in a Capri. Holding Diana's hand in the back of the car, Charles jokingly remarked that it looked like Bodie and Doyle of TV series *The Professionals* had joined the Royal Protection Squad.

After nearly nine hours labour, Diana delivered a healthy blue-eyed boy. But Charles was disappointed. He had wanted his second child to be a girl.

'Oh, it's a boy,' he said, 'and he's even got rusty hair.'

Diana's biographer Andrew Morton wrote: 'With these dismissive remarks he left to play polo.' For Diana this was a hammer blow to her already failing marriage.

'Something inside me closed off,' she said. 'By then I knew he had gone back to his lady but somehow we'd managed to have Harry.'

According to Harry, his father, 'Pa', said to 'Mummy' on the day of his birth: 'Wonderful! Now you've given me an heir and a spare—my work is done.'

This was presumably a joke. 'After delivering this bit of high comedy, Pa was said to have gone off to meet his girlfriend.' That is, the wicked Camilla, now Queen Consort. Though Diana knew all about Camilla, she insisted that Harry was 'born out of love'.

'Then,' she told Charles's former lover Lady 'Kanga' Tryon over a 'tiddly' (boozy) lunch at San Lorenzo, 'suddenly as Harry was born it just went bang, our marriage, the whole thing went down the drain.'

Outside the delivery room, crowds thronged the streets. The occasion was marked by two forty-one-gun salutes—one from Hyde Park nearby, the other from the Tower of London—and a town crier, decked out in a white-plumed hat and red breeches, who rang a large bronze bell and announced:

'Her Royal Highness the Princess Diana has issued forth a second son.'

Adding to the farce, it turned out that the town crier was improvised. It had been hired by a Japanese television company to give colour to their coverage.

Charles emerged from the hospital to shake hands with well-wishers. When a comely nineteen-year-old subject tried to kiss him, Charles pulled away, saying: 'I've had enough excitement for one day.' He then told the crowd that his new-born son as 'absolutely marvellous', adding disingenuously: 'It didn't matter whether it was a boy or a girl.'

The crowd chanted: 'Let's have another one.' Charles merely smiled and said: 'We've nearly got a full polo team now.'

He celebrated with an impromptu champagne party from the back of a Land Rover at a polo match hastily organised to celebrate the event. Camilla's position is not known.

Otherwise, 1984 was not a good year in Britain. The country was amid a divisive miners' strike. The old manufacturing industries were giving way to a modern economy reliant on financial services and banking, and unemployment had peaked at over three million, or 11.9% of the labour force.

But for one brief, bright moment, Harry's birth was seen as an excuse for national celebration, a short respite from the encircling gloom. Church bells rang, champagne corks popped, and flowers and telegrams of congratulation poured into the hospital. No scowling republican was heard to carp about another royal mouth to feed. The only sour face in the country was that of Arthur Scargill, the miners' leader who was leading them to disaster. When told that the new baby was to be named Henry, he said: 'Thank God, it's not Ian'—referring to Ian MacGregor, who Mrs Thatcher, the prime minister, had appointed to be Scargill's nemesis at the National Coal Board.

William Hill were also pleased. They had made George the 6-4 favourite and had not taken a single bet on Henry, a 50-1 outsider. The child would, of course, be Harry to family and friends—indeed, years later to the whole world.

The next day, there were over a thousand spectators in the streets of Paddington when Charles arrived with two-year-old William, who was going to see his baby brother for the first time. When Diana heard her toddler running down the corridor, she got out of bed and said softly: 'Wills, darling, come here.' Then the royal family had a moment alone and William was allowed to touch his brother and hold his hand.

'It will be lovely for William to have a companion and a playmate, and someone to fight with,' said Diana's father, Earl Spencer, as he hoisted the family standard above his Northamptonshire estate.

Two hours later, Diana emerged from the hospital to a cheering crowd, waving flags and the machine-gun stutter of the shutters of the paparazzi's cameras. The infant was cradled in her arms and Harry was a hit with the public from day one. Once they got home, Charles left Diana alone with the baby and zipped off in his Aston Martin to another polo match.

Was there any hope of Harry becoming less of a mummy's boy?

Left behind at Kensington Palace, Diana was not alone. She had nanny Barbara Barnes and her assistant-nanny Olga Powell to look after the two children. And the new baby was well provided for. According to *People* magazine, Diana was a compulsive shopper and, with a weekly budget of over £25,000 tax free, she had spent many hours in Harrods, picking up baby supplies such as towels and a new crib, bedecked with pink satin ribbons. The baby also had a new wardrobe. There would be no hand-me-downs from Wills.

Diana now had a delicate balancing act to perform. As she intended to breastfeed Harry, she was determined that William would not feel put out or neglected. On the other hand, as the second son, she was also determined that Harry would not suffer.

'Royal first-borns may get all the glory,' she said, 'but the second-borns enjoy more freedom. Only when Harry is a lot older will he realise how lucky he is not to have been the eldest. My second child will never have quite the same sort of pressure that poor William must face all his life.'

Oh, if she were alive to tell him that now.

Pride and Privilege

Andrew's mother was already Queen when he was born, and she and Prince Philip were holding the fort (for half a century as it would turn out). Harry's parents' job, by contrast, was much less glamorous. Di and Charles just had to look handsome and do as they were told. It was a waiting game that an army of junior royals had lived up to, or down, for centuries with greater and lesser success.

The palace was also a brilliant setting for crushing egos. Prince Philip famously described himself as 'a bloody amoeba' when his first two children did not get his surname. His family was as royal as it could get and he should have known what was in store.

Diana's pedigree by contrast wasn't quite as royal as Philip's. Even so, her family were Buckingham Palace insiders and had witnessed most if not all of the drill in recent times. She was the daughter of Frances Ruth Roche, daughter of the fourth Baron Fermoy and Viscount Althorp, later the eighth Earl Spencer, who was equerry to both George VI and Elizabeth II. Both her grandmothers, along with several great aunts, had been ladies-in-waiting to the Queen Mother. When her parents got married in Westminster Abbey, their wedding guests included the Queen, the Queen Mother, the Duke of Edinburgh and Princess Margaret. Diana's older sister, Sarah, was the goddaughter of the Queen Mother, while her younger brother Charles was the godson of the Queen.

While Harry's royal line on the male side is supposed to go back to William the Conqueror in 1066 through Charles, it really only goes back to the 1714, when a distant relative from the House of Hanover took the throne after Queen Anne. Although ostensibly a nursery teacher's assistant, Lady Di's British line was longer. They claimed descent from the ancient house of le Despencer—though this has been disputed—and Althorp in Northamptonshire has been their family seat for five hundred years. All these ancestral stories matter terribly after you've drunk the palace cool-aid, but can also bring you sharply down to earth.

As children, Diana and her siblings would play with Prince Andrew and Prince Edward when they visited the family estate at Park House, not far from the Queen's Norfolk home at Sandringham. The princes were of a similar age. But as a schoolgirl, she kept a picture of their older brother Charles pinned above her bed and she admitted to a childhood friend: 'I would love to be the Princess of Wales.' After meeting Charles on a visit to her older sister Sarah at Althorp when she was sixteen, she made sure to protect her virginity—just in case.

'I knew I had to keep myself tidy for what was ahead,' she told her biographer Andrew Morton.

Diana had been Prince Andrew's sweetheart when they were children, but when she met Charles again at a barbecue in July 1980 all that was soon history. When Charles brought Diana to Balmoral for royal approval Andrew and Edward merely got to compete to sit next to her at picnics. She was on the road to becoming a proper princess.

There followed the fairy-tale marriage at St Paul's Cathedral with an estimated 750 million people watching on TV worldwide. The church was packed with 3,500 royals and other dignitaries. Diana's wedding dress alone cost £9,000—£32,000 at today's prices—and the tiara she wore was a Spencer family heirloom. After a reception at Buckingham Palace, they honeymooned on board the royal yacht *Britannia*.

Within three months, Diana was pregnant and her popularity continued to grow. After she gave birth to William, Charles proved a doting father, though Diana already knew that his old love Camilla was lurking the background and tried to ignore her presence.

'I can't remember much,' she told Andrew Morton. 'I've blotted it out, it was such pain.'

This was the ambivalent situation that Harry found himself born into. Parents whose job was to circle a holding pen with countless other royals, not least of them Charles's spare Andrew.

Harry's life as spare was a little bit more crowded in other ways, too. Whereas Andrew was chauffeured to and fro Buckingham Palace to the Queen's royal residences, Harry's surroundings were more mundane. But only just.

The family lived in a spacious apartment in Kensington Palace, surrounded by tapestries, oil paintings, marble fireplaces and antique furniture. Unlike the many nurseries Andrew had enjoyed, 'Willy' and 'Harold' were largely consigned to the children's suite on the top floor, decorated by upmarket Dragons of Walton Street, specialists in 'luxury hand-painted children's furniture'.

Charles was happy for his children to be brought up out of sight by royal nannies, as he had been himself. As a life-long fan of the *Goon Show*, he saw his job as father as visiting the nursery to amuse them by pulling faces and putting on silly voices.

From the moment she married, Diana became a fully paid-up member of 'The Firm,' as Prince Philip put it. But she worried that she might be neglecting the boys by handing them to nannies. Determined to bring up her sons as normal children, she broke the royal tradition with Harry, inviting the butler, the housekeeper, her dressers, and the kitchen staff for drinks in the sitting room to meet the new addition to the family.

Although Charles remained stand-offish, Diana insisted. It was their sons one shot to have contact with people outside royal circles. Diana later said that it was really the first disagreement they had in their marriage and that this more than the presence of Camilla in the background would fester.

Christened Henry Charles Albert David, in St George's Chapel, Windsor, that December, Harry wore a 143-year-old christening. Unlike his mother, whose surname was Spencer, Harry as a top-tier HRH did not have a surname. Holy water was flown in from the river Jordan for the baptism. The service was conducted by the Archbishop of Canterbury and six godparents were on hand. William, however, objected to not being the centre of attention and played up. Everyone laughed and no one told him off. The whole ceremony was filmed and broadcast with the Queen's Christmas message a few days later to show that royal sibling rivalry was the same as in ordinary families.

Was Harry's a birth more ordinary than Andrew? Singer Barry Manilow gave Harry a five-inch grand piano as a christening present, while the poet laureate Ted Hughes contributed with a poem called 'Rain Charm for the Duchy: Devout Drench for the Christening of His Royal Highness Prince Harry'—a paean to the rivers of the West Country originally intended for his earlier *River* collection which some considered a little lazy.

Still, Diana continued to try and tone down the royal atmosphere of privilege. For Harry his mother and father were Mummy and Pa. The Queen was Granny, Prince Philip Grandpa and the Queen Mother Gran Gran. This informality did not sit naturally with the older royals steeped in rigid palace codes of conduct. Andrew still bowed to his mother before giving her a peck on the cheek. Naturally, they favoured William as heir apparent. This attitude was contagious at court. The boys' royal protection offer was shocked when staff simply ignored Harry when he suffered from carsickness.

Even Charles disapproved of some of Diana's efforts, especially when she took them out to McDonald's and the cinema. After all, they had one at home. She also took them on the bus and tube, hiding their faces with large caps while disguising herself with a brown wig. But she could hardly disguise their royal-protection officers who stuck out around them like sore thumbs.

Unsure of his place in the world, as a child, Harry turned to his father for re-assurance. 'Who am I?' he asked. Charles explained that, as well as being a little boy who played with toy soldiers that his parents loved, he was Prince Henry of Wales, third in line to the thrones of the United Kingdom, Australia, Canada, New Zealand, Papua New Guinea, the Solomon Islands, Tuvalu, the Bahamas, Belize, Jamaica, Antigua and Barbuda, Barbados, Grenada, St Kitts and Nevis, St Lucia and St Vincent and the Grenadines. He was also third in line to be the Supreme Governor of the Church of England, was to be addressed as 'Your Royal Highness' and would one day be a duke as well as a prince. Though it was a free geography lesson, as reassurances go, it evidently failed to hit the mark.

The only real freedom the children knew was within the walls of castles and palaces, or on the grounds of their private estates. Not shabby, but still far from ordinary. At Highgrove, Charles's country estate, he would encourage the boys to ride behind the Beaufort Hunt on their bicycles. Otherwise, they ran free in the extensive gardens and the nursery wing. But, as estate was his and not Diana's, on his orders his sons were kept away from the four reception rooms, nine bedrooms, six bathrooms and the staff quarters. When Charles was not outdoors overseeing the garden and his organic farm, he was in his library. It was sacrosanct and only pen-friendly (Charles would only turn on pens as king). The floor was littered with books, papers, and magazines. Nothing was to be touched. A maid was told that, if there was a pen on the floor, she must hoover around it.

As the schism between Harry's parents grew, Charles took to sleeping in his dressing room with his battered childhood teddy bear. Diana, too, comforted herself with cuddly toys. It was all very grown up. They were not to be disturbed in the morning and the children were given their breakfast in the nursery. The frosty atmosphere had its effect. Harry took to sucking his thumb, throwing food around and scribbling on the walls with crayon. Was it the first stirring of his illustrious literary career as an autobiographer?

Then there was the inevitable sibling rivalry. Family holidays were taken at Balmoral. The boys would travel there on the royal yacht *Britannia* before it was decommissioned in 1997. Harry's first birthday party was held on board and the family snaps were taken by Prince Andrew, a photo fiend before he had a media run-in with photographs. That autumn the press was allowed into Kensington Palace to photograph William and Harry. The heir, it was noted, was bossy with his little spare.

But to others Harry stood up for himself. When his nanny, an old-fashioned disciplinarian Olga Powell reprimanded him, Harry would say to his sixty-year-old carer: 'Go to your room, Olga.' His campaign of subversiveness worked. She was replaced by Ruth Wallace, a more *laissez-faire* nanny to Diana's liking. But scandal soon followed when Charles was angered when Ruth came down to breakfast wearing… jeans. Andrew was to replay this scenario in his Swiss chalet. A young guest was making tea in the morning the politely asked, 'Andrew, would you like a cup?' when their host walked in.

'I'm Prince Andrew to you,' snapped the royal, and walked off.

Ruth stayed on though. After three years in her post, she was replaced by Jessie Webb. When Harry was rude to her, he had to be admonished by Diana, as well as his royal protection officer Inspector Ken Wharfe.

Soon another dust-up followed. Wharfe in turn suffered Charles' wrath when he corrected the princes who persisted in pronouncing 'out' as 'ite'. William insisted that his way was correct, because that was the way his father pronounced the word, and Wharfe was upbraided for giving the royals elocution lessons.

As the marriage fell apart, all these attempts at having Harry and William grow up a little less royal were getting complicated.…

Band of Brothers

While William toed the line, Harry grew up more mischievous like his fellow spare Andrew, but with less of a line in embarrassing the staff at home with practical jokes. When Harry began at Mrs Mynors' infant academy in nearby Chepstow Villas at the age of three, Inspector Wharfe would report back regarding his antics, frequently leaving Diana helpless with laughter. One morning at assembly, Harry kept tugging at the music teacher Mr Pritchard's trousers while he was trying to play the piano. Finally, Pritchard lost his temper and told him to stop, but Harry piped up: 'But Mr Pritchard, I can see your willy.' Mentioning his groin was to become Harry's thing.

As the royal couple drifted apart, royal duties kept Diana busy and the two boys would have breakfast with one or other of their parents. Sometimes even dinner. The boys' protection officers were left to organise picnic and games of football. Occasionally, though, as they grew up. With the staff, the boys were boisterous, regularly challenging Wharfe to a fight.

'One would go for my head,' he said, 'and the other would attack my more sensitive parts, landing punches towards my groin, which, if they connected, would make me kneel over in agony.' Freud would have something to say about the boys venting their aggression as the tension between their parents grew.

If Charles was on hand, he would pop his head round the door and ask: 'They're not being too much bother, are they Ken?'

'No, sir, not at all,' Wharfe would say breathlessly as he recovered. There was nothing they could not get away with.

'William was likeable, but capable of being quite sly,' said Wharfe. 'He would choose to attack from behind as a child, whereas Harry would always grab your nuts.

The boys would also fight and sometimes William would bully his little brother.

'But Harry didn't really have a problem with that because he could fight his own corner,' Wharfe said. 'Very often he was on top of the game and had to be remonstrated by the nannies and pulled off.'

Of the two, Harry was always more troublesome. Housekeeper Wendy Berry also recalled that, while William would ask her for 10p, Harry would always insist on 20p. They had yet to learn that royals don't carry cash.

Diana's campaign to have the boys mingle with ordinary people was otherwise flagging. In summer, when the family had barbecues by the pool, the boys would soak the royal protection officers with their water pistols. When they had got them as a present that Christmas, they sneaked out to give the chefs a soaking. As with Andrew's pranks as a child, it was completely hilarious because they were princes.

When William tried to restrain his younger brother, Harry would say: 'I can do what I like because I'm not going to be king. You can't because you are.'

Diana tried to manage Harry's backhanded complaint by calling her younger son GKH, 'Good King Harry'. This recalled, particularly, Henry VIII and Henry V, the victor of Agincourt. While eschewing any knowledge of Shakespeare, during his time spent in combat in Afghanistan Harry talked of going 'unto the breach' from Henry's rallying speech in *Henry V*, omitting the somewhat charged: 'Cry "God for Harry, England, and Saint George!"'

Like Andrew, Harry was also the more media-prone of the two boys. After his first day at Mrs Mynors', he emerged holding loo-roll binoculars to his eyes, looking out for the paparazzi. William told him: 'Don't ever talk to the 'tographers, right. Don't trust 'tographers.' Charles would have said exactly the same about the press. But like Andrew, while William would pull his cap down, Harry would pull faces—a trick he would repeat on formal occasions despite being admonished by his mother. Even now he does not trust the ''tographers'—unless they are on staff. Andrew of course has little staff left.

Granny's Little Soldier

When their parents' marriage fell apart, the boys found that the house was a little bigger. They were allowed downstairs after their evening bath to relate their day's adventures to 'Mummy's friend', Major James Hewitt. Harry was particularly taken with this dashing cavalry officer as he was one of 'Granny's soldiers'. While William spent his time doing games and puzzles, Harry preferred playing with soldiers and he had a model of a German Panzer tank in his nursery in Highgrove. Hewitt had the regimental tailor run up a little camouflage uniform for Harry that he never took off. It came with a mini-flak jacket. This was long before he was to get the uniform to go with his Panzer.

From the beginning, Harry was enthralled by 'Uncle James's' tales of army life. Hewitt took Harry to Combermere Barracks, home of the Household Cavalry. There young Harry clambered on a tank and announced: 'I'm going to be a soldier when I grow up.' He even carried out 'missions' on the grounds of Kensington Palace.

One day he persuaded Wharfe to let him play with a police two-way radio. The prince's 'assignment' was to go to the police officer at the gate, then report back. When no report came back, Wharfe tried to reach him, but Harry failed to respond.

Eventually, the call came: 'Ken, this is Harry'. Wharfe could hear traffic in the background.

'Where are you?' asked Wharfe.

'I'm outside Tower Records on the High Street,' came the reply. It was his first attempt to escape palace life.

Like Uncle Andrew, Harry was interested in guns. 'Can we see your gun, Ken?' he would ask Wharfe.

'No,' Wharfe replied. 'You only take a gun out of its holster if you intend to use it.'

In Andrew's case, his father Prince Philip and the 11-year-older Prince

Charles when in uniform had been his role models. But at this time in Harry's life, Prince Charles was in his treehugging phase and William not much older than he and not really a role model. In fact, William's father-figure seems to have been their protection officer Wharfe. Like him, he wanted to become a policeman. And so Harry's role model were his mother's friends, mainly Hewitt. Like Andrew when growing up as spare, Harry was attracted to the simplicity of having a clear enemy and being licensed to shoot them to smithereens.

Thanks to Hewitt, both Harry and William had unlimited access to army equipment. He arranged for them to visit army camps in Wiltshire. When Hewitt was posted abroad, Harry was inconsolable. Hewitt and Diana's relationship was not to last in any case. Hewitt had a reputation as an accomplished womaniser. One girlfriend nicknamed him 'Timeshare'. Another jokingly referred to him as 'the mounted cavalry' and said that a night with him was like 'having been shagged by the entire 17/21st Lancers'.

In Harry's eyes, Diana's other boyfriends could never compare. Her next lover, James Gilbey, was 'no fun', and later on, Dr Hasnat Khan was polite and pleasant, but he was no swashbuckling warrior.

Throughout his life, Harry was dogged by the canard that James Hewitt was his father, a rumour based on the fact that they both sported ginger hair. Before Harry went to Eton, Charles sought to counter the cruel gossip that was bound to circulate, assuring him that Hewitt, by then a real-life hero as a tank commander in the First Gulf War, was not his father.

Harry thanked Charles, but the rumour persisted. As late as 2002, when Harry was eighteen, Hewitt was forced to release a public statement announcing that, contrary to recurring speculation, he was not Harry's father, insisting that he had not meet Diana until Harry was a toddler.

Even this did not squash the rumours. A friend of Charles's who also knew Hewitt told the *Daily Mail*: 'I know what the official line is, but I still find the resemblance extraordinary. Quite recently I was at a table with James Hewitt and, never mind his hair, when you look into his eyes it's like you are looking into Harry's. There is not a scintilla of difference.'

Wharfe also denied the rumour in 2003 when he wrote the book *Diana: Closely Guarded Secret*. In it, he said: 'The malicious rumours that still persist about the paternity of Prince Harry used to anger Diana greatly. The nonsense should be scotched here and now. Harry was born on 15 September 1984. Diana did not meet James until the summer of 1986, and the red hair, gossips so love to cite as proof is, of course, a Spencer trait.'

Even so, Harry continued to hero-worship Hewitt until he tried to sell

Countryside Yuletide

Andrew only ever wanted to be Prince Andrew, well King Andrew secretly anyway. Wills wanted to become a policeman. Harry, in *Spare*, in turn recorded his youthful ambition to become a fondue attendant in Lech, since his mother loved fondue, or a ski instructor. When he first accompanied his family on their annual visit to the Swiss ski resort of Klosters, he ignored the ski instructor and took off down hill, only to plough onto grass and crash into a chalet. He evidently still had a lot to learn. Still, it was pretty accurate guide to the future. Spare Andrew was happy wallowing where he was. William was getting ready for the top job, and spare Harry wanted to get away from it all with skates on.

While Diana indulged the boys' passion for action with Indiana Jones movies, Charles sought to hook them on the finer details of gardening, though left to his own devices, Harry would have preferred to play soldiers. Once, when Charles, was on his way to an official function, Harry ambushed him, Andrew-style. After a tussle, Charles had to delay the royal helicopter and trudge back to the house to clean up.

'Look at me,' he complained. 'I'm absolutely covered in sheep shit.'

Even still, the boys were exposed to the robust joys of hunting, shooting and fishing. Harry recalls that the summer would end with the family gathering at Balmoral where the boys would get to play with the other royal children and explore the 50,000-acres of woodlands that stretched as far as the eye could see. It was there that they were taught the finer arts of catching salmon, stalking deer, and shooting rabbits. Diana, despite having a preference for city life, would often take the boys to their other grandmother's country retreat near Oban in Argyllshire. In happier times, the family would also holiday in Sandringham, Norfolk, on the Scilly Isles—part of their father's Duchy of Cornwall—or vacation in the king of Spain's palace in Majorca. These vast estates also offered a holiday away from mixing with commoners. The two boys would play with the four sons of millionaire racehorse owner Hugh van Custem, who rented Anmer Hall on the Sandringham estate, later the country home of William and Kate.

Traditionally, the royal family would celebrate Christmas at Windsor, but when Harry was young, the Queen changed the venue to Sandringham. There, the family would gather on Christmas Eve to exchange presents, each family member having their own table covered with a white linen tablecloth to amass their presents on. Harry's gifts usually followed a military theme, yet he still resents the year his great-aunt, Princess Margaret (another indulged spare), bought him a biro—like her nephew evidently much taken with pens—though he conceded it was nicely wrapped.

On Christmas morning, they would attend the church on the estate where the Queen, Prince Philip and Charles would each pop a £10 note into the collection. This, of course, had first been ironed and folded so that the Queen's head was outermost.

After acknowledging the small crowd that had gathered outside the church to pay their respects, the royal family would return to the house to prepare for a grand, formal family dinner. They drank from crystal glasses etched with the royal cipher EIIR and ate off plates bearing the monogram of the Queen's grandparents, George V and Queen Mary. According to royal tradition, the menus were in French—though the fare was the traditional turkey with all the trimmings and Christmas pudding. Afterwards, they gathered in the saloon to hear the Queen's speech. The formal festivities were followed by board games and charades. The family even played *Who Wants to be a Millionaire?*, though the game must have lost something of its edge as many already far richer, or just had to wait it out no questions asked.

Otherwise, they moved to the ballroom to watch a film. Harry's favourite was *Zulu* in which 150 British soldiers at Rorke's Drift held off more than 3000 Zulu warriors in 1879. Harry recalled visiting the site of the battle with his father. However, while condemning 'imperialism, colonialism, nationalism—in short, theft', he fails to mention the Battle of Isandlwana that happened on that very day six miles away. This is where over 20,000 British troops and auxiliaries armed with breechloading rifles and artillery were massacred by an equal number of Zulus carrying assegai spears, cowhide shields, and a handful of antiquated rifles. Perhaps the British getting a thrashing was not sufficiently significant.

Even fellow spare Andrew was a favourite of Harry's as he was in Britain on his few days off from his day job at the Royal Navy. Hard to imagine nowadays but Andrew was once more popular than Harry's mother Princess

Diana as a result of the Falklands War. Harry would get Uncle Andrew to tell him tales of derring-do from his time serving as a helicopter pilot when his warship came under attack of Exocet rockets and he had to do rescue missions or act as decoy. Later, Harry would sit beside an anxious Diana as she watched the news of the Gulf War in which Hewitt was serving.

On Boxing Day, there would be the inevitable shoot, with venison stew for lunch, followed by treacle tarts—another of Harry's favourites. But his active childhood took its toll. Just before his fourth birthday he was rushed to Great Ormond Street Hospital for an emergency hernia operation. Little did he know, this would not be the last of troubles with his lower abdomen.

What's in a Ball?

While Charles and Diana saw increasingly less of each other, the two boys grew closer, amusing themselves with mischief. At Highgrove, they built a go-kart track through Charles' vegetable patch. Harry also wanted it to run across the lawn which would cut the grass up.

'We can't do that because Papa will go mad,' said William.

'It doesn't matter about that,' said Harry.

While Harry was mischievous, he was also friendly and affectionate. Inspector Wharfe compared him to a Labrador. 'If someone took him off and gave him some food, he would go,' Wharfe said. When William went to boarding school at Ludgrove in Berkshire, Harry found himself aimlessly wandering the palace without his two-years-older partner in crime. He had his parents to himself—one at a time, of course. He enjoyed this. But without William he was sometimes lonely. He would wander into the kitchen and asked the staff if he could help. The chef would give him some menial task to do, like beating an egg, and he would soon get bored and move on. No matter what Wharfe thought, since his marriage to Meghan, it is thought by some that Harry has become a lapdog.

Harry must have realised, even as a young boy, that something was wrong in the family. He would often be farmed out to the Beaufort Polo Club when things were bad at home and learnt to play polo from an early age. It was another must-have life skill for a royal. And a good place for royals to make friends. He and William spent time with the three young children of Simon and Claire Tomlinson who ran the Beaufort Polo Club. But, while Diana was usually good at hiding her distress, Harry would sometimes find her crying.

Even at the age of seven, there were royal duties to perform. He and William had to join his parents on a royal visit to Canada. In March 1992, they went skiing, but the trip was tinged with tragedy when news came that Diana's father had died. After the funeral, Diana took the boys on holiday to Necker, courtesy of Richard Branson who owned the exclusive Caribbean

Island. There was still fun to be had, too. Harry and William hatched a plan to bombard an intruding paparazzi with water balloons, but the two brothers got into a fight which ended with Harry throwing a snooker ball William. He later got into the habit of hurling balls at his brother, not to mention at the paparazzi and the public. Perhaps the lapdog has some balls after all.

Colditz in Kilts

While William and Harry were sent, predictably, to Eton, the poshest school in England (and the school Charles wasn't allowed to go to by his father), Andrew had been sent to Gordonstoun, a strict boarding school in the north of Scotland. The school's founder had originally set up camp in Nazi Germany, when Prince Phillip attended, but, being Jewish, decamped to Scotland before the war. Charles, a shy and sensitive lad and somewhat of an intellectual, was teased and bullied by his peers for whom the institute was mainly a finishing school in living rough before the luxury of a well-heeled inheritance beckoned. He hated it and called it 'Colditz in kilts'. When Andrew arrived, Gordonstoun had let its hair down a bit, or at any rate had introduced some creature comforts including girls as the school had just gone co-ed.

Andrew was neither strong in academics nor in sport, yet he was good at having a large ego. Other pupils called him 'boastful' and 'big headed'. One said: 'He had a bit of the 'I am the Prince' about him when he arrived. He soon had it knocked out of him. The ribbings he got were unmerciful.' Like Charles, Andrew recounted his time at his *alma mater*: 'The beds are hard and it's all straw mattresses, bread and water—just like a prison.'

But, unlike his older brother, it didn't matter to Andrew what other people thought of him. Criticism was like water of a duck's back. Frankly, his attention span was only barely wide enough to cover himself. In true lad fashion, Andrew regaled his classmates with crude and offensive jokes, earning himself the nickname 'The Sniggerer'. One student recalled: 'By the time he's finished a joke he's laughing so much you can't understand the punch line.'

Neither of his parents felt the need to trouble his mind with the thought that he shouldn't grow up as a royal. During the holidays, he indulged in the stipulated round of Windsor luxuries– learning to ski in Switzerland, visiting his cousins in Germany, sailing on the royal yacht *Britannia,* and learning to fly at RAF Milltown.

At sixteen, he went with his parents to the Montreal Olympics where girls began to take an interest in him too. Charles conceded that Andrew was the 'one with the Robert Redford looks'. One Canadian newspaper called him 'six foot of sex appeal'. He was bombarded with requests for dates, invitations to parties and telephone numbers.

This boosted his already sky-high ego. He flirted with the female competitors in the Olympic village and took a shine to his minder, a bubbly blonde named Sandi Jones, saying: 'Call me Andrew, not your royal highness.' Flirtation disguised as a rare instance of diluting court protocol. His name was also connected with that of Silvia Sommerlath, who had been a hostess at the 1972 Munich Olympics. However, she married his cousin in Sweden, Carl XVI Gustaf, and became queen in 1976. Andrew had once again come second to an heir.

When Andrew returned to Canada in 1977 to attend Lakefield College School near Toronto, dozens or young girls turned out at the airport. They screamed, blew kisses, and chanted: 'We want Andy.' It was enough to turn any young man's head. Certainly, Andrew didn't have to make the slightest effort.

When he played rugby at Lakefield, girls turned out on the touchline to cheer for his every move, wearing jumpers emblazed with the slogans 'I'm an Andy Windsor girl' and 'Andy King'. Canada was like being part of a royal Tinder where all he had to do was click 'like'. He invited Sandi Jones to the school dance and they danced cheek to cheek. This did not go down well with the other girls. Schoolgirl Patricia Foy complained: 'It was unfair that he had one girl all the time. A lot of us wanted to dance with him.' In a school production of *Oliver*, he tried to revive the stricken Nancy. 'My heartbeat shot up to about a hundred miles an hour when he put his fingers on my wrist,' said Gillian Wilson who was playing the part. He had a similar effect on the teenage Linda Sergeant who bumped into him while jogging on the college playing fields. 'He was a real charmer,' she said. 'I really fancied him.'

Surprisingly, given his current press, he was in his element and got a lot of likes back. At a party given for him at Government House in Ottawa, he spent the night dancing with star figure skater Lynn Nightingale, then teamed up again with Sandi Jones again for a tour of wildlife parks. In Vancouver on Canada day, he was cheered by bevies of young girls. At a rodeo hostess Gillie Newman called him: 'A real prince charming.'

Everyone thought, he had done a great job. Back home in Britain after his time abroad, at the age of eighteen, Andrew received his first handout from the state when parliament granted him £20,000 (then $50,000) a year, worth £100,000 now ($180,000). Predictably, did this little to improve his last year at Gordonstoun. Fellow pupil Lucilla 'Lulu' Houseman said: 'He didn't shine at anything. Well, not quite. He loved having a good time. In fact, the story that went round the school was that he failed some 'O' levels because he spent all his time reading trashy magazines and comics.' However, he left Gordonstoun under something of a cloud after his detective reported some of the boys for smoking cannabis.

While Andrew didn't inhale, when it was the adolescent Harry's turn, he did. Cocaine doesn't do much for him, he has volunteered. But he has admitted to smoking marihuana to deal with his messy past. Harry said, 'I started doing it recreationally and then started to realise how good it was for me, I would say it is one of the fundamental parts of my life that changed me and helped me deal with the traumas and pains of the past.' Either way it didn't make much of a difference for. Andrew spends his time filling 'trashy magazines', along with nephew Harry. Though Harry seems to do generate content for a living whereas his uncle seems merely haunted by headlines past.

Passion Killer

Both Andrew's father and elder brother had been made head boy, or 'guardian', at Gordonstoun. Andrew was pipped at the post by Georgina Houseman, the first girl to take the post. Second again.

However, he was a still success with the girls. Although the sex ratio was one girl to every two boys, he earned the nickname Randy Andy for his effortless conquests. What else is a spare to do in his spare time? The girls he took out became known as Andy's Harem. Lulu Houseman reported: 'He had several girlfriends at Gordonstoun as well as many friends who happened to be girls. His girlfriends were quite good for him because he took them fairly seriously and serious relationships are a steadying influence.'

The operative word here was 'fairly'. The first was Clio Nathaniels, the daughter of an architect who lived in the Bahamas. She left school unexpectedly and fled back to Nassau after he dropped her.

'Andrew was very embarrassed about the whole affair,' said Clio's mother and as she knows best we have to take her word for it.

He then turned his attentions to Clio's schoolfriend, eighteen-year-old Kirsty Richmond. He shared a love of tennis and skiing with her and they also wrote to each other during the holidays. Kirsty was a hit with the Queen and was invited to spend Christmas at Sandringham two years running. The other girls bitchily dismissed the affair, saying: 'It was just Kirsty's turn.' Besides Andrew was involved with another girl at Gordonstoun, an American beauty named Sue Garnard. According to school friends: 'She is Andrew's long-term girlfriend. She doesn't mind Andrew taking Kirsty home because she knows she is just a friend.' Even Steven, he also took Sue home to meet the Queen during the vacations.

In London, he spent time with heiress Julia Guinness usually in the posh nightclub Annabel's. 'He is a bit of a flirt but the most charming person you could hope to meet,' she said.

He also hung out at Tramp and Tokyo Joe's in Piccadilly. Newspapers began showing pictures of him emerging from nightspots with various blondes. The number of girlfriends attached to the prince of fun were multiplying, but as the paparazzi started circling him, it was no longer just Andrew who broke things off. His activities were inhibited by his police minder. 'He's a real passion killer, if you will pardon the phrase,' said one of his flames about the bodyguard that accompanied the prince.

Though he was charming to his girlfriends, he had already that disregard for the sensitivities of that he would display later. One of his first official duties was a 1988 visit to Lockerbie, where eleven people had died on the ground when Pan Am Flight 103 crashed on the town. He told the grieving locals that the disaster had been 'much worse' for the Americans and thought aloud that it had 'only been a matter of time' before a plane fell out of the sky.

He was no better with the employees. Royal protection officer Ken Wharfe said he was once moved from a window seat on a plane from Balmoral because he was obstructing Andrew's view. 'His manners,' Wharfe said, 'are just awful.'

An aide said: 'He treats his staff in a shocking, appalling way. He's been incredibly rude to his personal protection officers, literally throwing things on the ground and demanding they "fucking pick them up". No social graces at all. Sure, if you're a lady with blonde hair and big boobs, then I bet he is utterly charming.'

History was to cast some shade over that assertion.

Naughty Mummy

The peccadilloes of William and Harry's parents were kept from the public, at least until Andrew Morton's book *Diana: Her True Story* was published. In it she talked about the breakdown of her marriage and her battle with bulimia. Diana claimed that she had not collaborated in the writing of the book. But, as Harry says, the media are conveyor belts of lies. It soon became clear that she had indirectly given Morton everything he needed for a book.

To shield her children from the attendant publicity, Diana took them on a Caribbean cruise on board a luxurious four-hundred-foot yacht loaned to them by Greek shipping tycoon Yiannis Latsis. Harry would leap the thirty feet from the deck into the sea, daring his brother to do the same. They returned to England to the furore of 'Squidgygate' when *The Sun* published transcripts of private phone conversations between their mother and James Gilbey, a friend, soap actor and heir to a gin fortune.

Again, the boys were protected as much as possible. They were farmed out to family friends and, while William was at boarding school, access to newspapers and television was restricted. That September, Harry was shipped off to Ludgrove to join his brother. It was a family-run school that prided itself on being both relaxed and supportive. But the windows had to be bullet-proof, the doors reinforced, and royal protection officers stationed nearby. Otherwise, the boys were treated just like any other pupil and had to call the teachers 'Sir' or 'Ma'am'. Prayers were said in Latin or Greek. After chapel on Sundays, the boys could write home to their parents. In the afternoon, the headmaster showed old war movies in the refectory.

It was all change from now on. Three months after Harry had started at Ludgrove, Diana drove to the school to tell the boys that she and their father were separating. William and Harry were not surprised by the news and appeared unaffected. After they had been told, an announcement was made in parliament. There were no plans for divorce, Prime Minister John Major said, and both parents would both continue to participate fully in the upbringing of their children.

However, that Christmas there would be a major difference. Protocol demanded that the boys spend the holiday with their father as Sandringham, while Diana returned to her family home at Althorp. But for the New Year, they went with their mother to the island of Nevis in the Caribbean.

When they returned home, it was their father's turn to run for cover. The *Daily Mirror* was running the transcript of an excruciating erotic phone conversation between Charles and his future wife Camilla. This is the one where Charles says he wants to be reincarnated as a Tampax.

'My luck to be chucked down a lavatory and go on and on forever swirling around the top, never going down,' said Charles.

Charles moved out from Kensington Palace and into York House, a wing of St James's Palace. Diana then redecorated their apartments in a more modern style. Her bedroom was done out in pastel shades, with lace, frills and scented candles. Her New Age friends also 'cleansed' the palace to rid of bad spirits. Meanwhile Charles expunged all trace of Diana from Highgrove, redecorating with dark furniture and heavy curtains—a style she considered stuffy and old fashioned. It was abundantly clear to the boys that there was no love lost between their parents.

The rivalry to be the best parent soon started. Yet to be stripped of her royal duties, Diana was still colonel-in-chief of The Light Dragoons. Harry was given a new uniform when they went to inspect the regiment in Germany. He got to ride in Scimitar tanks and rattle out blank rounds on a machine gun. Another treat was a visit to the Metropolitan Police Firearms Training Unit where, again, he got to hold a gun. Charles competed by taking Harry to visit the Royal Engineers, the regiment that had held Rorke's Drift. The boys were also on public display at the celebrations marking the fiftieth anniversary of VE day and VJ day that ended World War II.

While what became the War of the Waleses raged, the boys found a safe haven among school friends at Ludgrove. In the holidays, William and Harry split their time between their parents. Home life with Diana became much more informal. Rather than being served at table, she told the chef to leave their dinner out on the sideboard, so the boys could serve themselves. When they were with their mother, they got to play with Andrew's children Beatrice and Eugenie, daughters of Sarah 'Fergie' Ferguson, duchess of York. Diana was always very fond of Andrew. When with Charles, the boys spent time with Peter and Zara Phillips, the children of Princess Anne.

Charles employed twenty-eight-year-old Tiggy Legge-Bourke to look after the boys. Another choice from the top shelf. Both her mother and her aunt were ladies-in-waiting to Princess Anne. She called William and Harry 'my babies'. Another fan of the Beaufort Hunt, she said: 'I give them what they need at this stage—fresh air, a rifle and a horse. She [Diana] gives them a tennis racket and a bucket of popcorn at the movies.' Diana gossiped to butler Paul Burrell that Charles was in love with Tiggy and intended to marry her. After a reported kiss on the slopes at Klosters, rumours that Tiggy and Charles were having an affair flared in the press, causing the boys fresh embarrassment. To Harry, this meant that Tiggy was Diana's spare.

Their parents' separation remained a matter of public debate when Diana appeared on *Panorama* and was interviewed by Martin Bashir. Harry was eleven then. Not only did Diana expose her marriage as a sham, she also showed the rest of the royal family up in a bad light. The Queen approved a divorce and stripped Diana of her title 'Her Royal Highness'. Her staff was cut, along with her charity work. However, she retained her patronage of the National AIDS Trust and Centrepoint, taking the boys to a homeless shelter where they played cards with rough sleepers.

Their mother was looking for a new love in her life. Diana's friend Jemima Khan told *Vanity Fair* that Diana was madly in love with Pakistani-born heart surgeon Hasnet Khan and wanted to marry him, even if it meant living in Pakistan. This would have been impossible, of course, because of the boys. Meanwhile Diana cut her ties with Andrew's wife Fergie, the Duchess of York, because in her autobiography she said she had caught a verruca from a pair of Diana's shoes. The Yorks clearly had a thing with feet. When Fergie's toe being sucked by one of her lovers was caught on camera, official divorce from Andrew, the duke of York, followed soon after.

Meanwhile, Tiggy was becoming closer with the boys. At the age of twelve, Harry was pictured shooting rabbits with Tiggy. William invited her to the Eton summer picnic instead of his parents. Diana was furious when she was seen smoking in front of the boys. Nevertheless, Tiggy went everywhere with them.

In *Spare*, Harry recalled with almost erotic relish being blooded by Tiggy after the first time he killed a rabbit. 'She dipped her long, slender fingers into the rabbit's body, under the flap of smashed fur, scooped out a dollop of blood and smeared it tenderly across my forehead, down my cheeks and nose. "Now", she said, in her throaty voice, "you are blooded."'

It gets worse. After he killed a deer, Tiggy slit open its belly and shoved Harry's head into it. After this bizarre rite, they stripped off and checked each other for lice which, according to Harry, 'often crawl up into your balls'.

Half-Mast

That summer, Harrods owner Mohamed al-Fayed, a generous donor to Diana's charities took pity on the princess, invited her and the boys to the South of France. They flew in al-Fayed's private jet to his summer home overlooking St Tropez. They later moved on to al-Fayed's £15-million yacht *Jonikal.* This attracted the attention of the paparazzi, who hired a helicopter to follow them. Charles was not to be outdone. After ten days, the boys returned to England, where they embarked on a cruise round the Western Isles with Charles on *Britannia*—the last trip before the royal yacht was decommissioned—before fetching up, as usual, at Balmoral.

After cruising around the Greek Islands, Diana herself returned to London to break it off with Dr Hasnat Khan. She then paid al-Fayed's son Dodi a visit on the *Jonikal*, which was moored off Sardinia. They were to return to London together, but made a brief visit to the Ritz in Paris. On their way to Dodi's apartment in Rue Arsene Houssaye, the car they were riding in crashed in the tunnel under the Pont de l'Alma. Dodi died on the spot. Diana died in hospital two hours later. The royal soap opera had turned into tragedy.

Charles heard the news that night. At 7.15am the following morning, he woke William. Together they went to break the news to Harry. Later, Harry was driven to the nearby church, Crathie Kirk. Crowds gathered to offer their condolences. As Harry left the church, he asked Tiggy Legge-Bourke: 'Are you sure Mummy is dead?' There had been no mention of Tiggy at the service.

Charles could not stay to comfort his grieving sons. He had to fly to Paris to bring Diana's body back. In the national hysteria that followed her death, their grandmother the Queen was criticised for not having a flag flown at half-mast on Buckingham Palace for her daughter-in-law and the mother of the heir and spare. Buckingham Palace said it would be a breach of protocol. It was also noted that she had not spoken publicly in tribute to Diana. But, for the Queen, bereavement was a private matter.

Prime Minister Tony Blair lent a hand, organising a state funeral and dubbing the blue-blooded Diana 'the People's Princess'. The Queen gave in and paid tribute to Diana on television—only the second time she had addressed the nation outside her Christmas broadcasts. 'This week at Balmoral we have all been trying to help William and Harry come to terms with the devastating loss that they and the rest of us have suffered,' she said.

Harry was seen outside the gates of Balmoral with Charles, reading the messages on the floral tributes to his mother. He then accompanied the Duke of Edinburgh, Charles, William, and Diana's brother Charles, walking behind her coffin as it was pulled on a gun carriage from the Chapel Royal to Westminster Abbey. On top of the coffin were a bunch of white freesias and an envelope with 'Mummy' written on it in Harry's handwriting. Inside the Abbey, Harry broke down.

Elton John played 'Candle in the Wind', and, in his eulogy, Charles Spencer blamed the paparazzi for Diana's death and pledged that her 'blood family' would rally around to protect the boys. The sentiment was applauded by the crowds outside—and by Harry, William and Charles. The Queen, the *Daily Mail* reported, was angry. Prince Philip and the Queen Mother disapproved.

Diana was buried at Althorp. Afterwards, Harry and Williams returned to Highgrove with their father, where Tiggy was waiting. Then, after a quick visit to Kensington Palace to collect mementoes from their home with their mother, they headed for the Beaufort Hunt. Four days after the funeral, the boys were back at school.

Everyone Will Think He's Stupid

When twelve-year-old Harry returned to school at Ludgrove after Diana's death, he was quieter and more thoughtful. He had to study hard to pass his common entrance exam to get into Eton. 'If he doesn't go there, everyone will think he's stupid,' Diana had said. But there were distractions. On his thirteenth birthday, Diana's sister, Lady Sarah McCorquodale, gave Harry the PlayStation Diana had bought for him in Paris. In *Spare*, Harry said it was an Xbox, but it did not come out until four years after her death. This was one of the factual mistakes that pedants have picked up on as misremembered by the 38-year-old in *Spare*.

The situation at their father's home was not much better. The public had taken Diana's side against Charles and blamed Camilla for the breakup of their marriage. Camilla stopped visiting Highgrove for a while and Charles tried to console Harry. At half-term, he had official duties in Africa and took his youngest along. He and Tiggy went on a safari in Botswana and, in South Africa, he met Nelson Mandela and the Spice Girls. As icing on the cake of the soldier wannabee, Charles then took him to Rorke's Drift.

Later, Charles tried to ease Camilla into his sons' lives. The emotional blackmail was Charles's lonely teddy bear. Didn't their father deserve a proper companion, Harry tells us? The rest is history. As part of the strategy, her two children, Tom and Laura, were invited to stay in Birkhall, a property in Scotland belonging to the Queen Mother, which Charles would later inherit. William and Harry then met with Camilla privately to plan a surprise party for Charles's fiftieth birthday. Guests included Stephen Fry, Rowan Atkinson and Emma Thompson who were persuaded to stage comedy sketches poking fun at their father. But Harry complained in *Spare* that she was leaking their private conversations to firm up her position.

Top DJs, who Charles had never heard of, were employed. When 'YMCA' by the Village People came on, the boys encouraged Charles to do some dance moves. Finally, in his cups, Harry stripped stark naked and streaked among the guests. A red-faced Charles excused his son's behaviour as 'teenage high spirits' and said that he had done much the same at his age. No one believed him.

The following summer Camilla was firmly installed in their lives when Charles, Camilla and the four children holidayed on the *Alexandros*. A drunken Harry was sometimes found weeping the arms of Tiggy. He abseiled down the Grwyne-Fawr dam in Monmouthshire without protective gear. Charles upbraided Tiggy, but Harry leapt to her defence. In April 1999, fourteen-year-old Harry returned to Botswana for another safari with Tiggy. This time Mark Dyer, a former Welsh Guards officer who had been Charles' equerry, rather than Charles was with them. Tiggy was soon to leave Charles' service to get married. It was said that, at her reception, Harry swallowed a goldfish that had been part of the table decorations, but apparently, he remained fully clothed. In 2023, Harry was to complain that his step-mother Camilla had been leaking their private conversations to firm up her position.

On the first Mother's Day following Diana's death, William and Harry laid flowers on her grave at Althorp, despite Charles' trepidation. He cancelled a long-standing engagement to take Harry to France to watch England in the World Cup instead. As a result, David Beckham became Harry's latest hero.

The boys were in two minds about the memorial service being held to mark the anniversary of their mother's death. Harry persuaded William attend on the understanding that it would mark the end of the public mourning. For Harry there would be no end. He later complained on NBC that, since Diana had died, they had never been allowed any peace and quiet, and that her face was still splashed over the newspapers all the time. True, in part, she had been canonised by some papers.

When the fourteen-year-old Harry joined William at Eton that autumn, a statement was issued on their behalf, saying: 'They believe their mother would want people to move on—because she would have known that constant reminders of her death can create nothing but pain to those left behind. They therefore hope very much that their mother and her memory will now finally be able to rest in peace.'

At Eton, Harry joined William in Manor House, the most prestigious of the school's twenty-five houses. With Charles in charge of their education, mixing with ordinary people was well and truly off the table. Harry made some good friends at Eton. These included Ton 'Skippy' Inskip, the son of a banker and field master at, you guessed it, the Beaufort Hunt, and Guy Pelly, usually described as a 'London aristocrat', both of whom would become Harry's partners in crime in his later tabloid excesses. Not that he was not able to get into trouble on his own. He got into a number of playground scrapes and was known for his aggression on the football field. The Palace had to plead with newspaper editors not to print pictures of him when he was more than a little unruly out and about on the streets of Eton and Windsor, though they did run a photograph of Harry on crutches after he had kicked in a window during a dispute with another boy over a girl they both fancied.

He indulged in the usual comic-book pranks of balancing a book on the top of a door so that it fell on a teacher's head, and he jumped out from behind a tree pretending to be an autograph hunter when William was running a cross-country race, losing him first place. But there was more going on. 'Harry was like a firecracker,' said one teacher. 'When other pupils saw him coming, they used to pass a by-now familiar warning: "Don't light the blue touch paper". In other words: don't give him the slightest excuse to vent his spleen.'

Like the older spare Andrew, Harry never excelled academically. Instead he, too, went down the career path as a prince of fun. By age sixteen, he was house captain of games and had represented the school at cricket, polo and rugby. He was also an enthusiastic player of the Eton wall game and an Arsenal supporter. Some of his aggression he unleashed when he discovered Eton's Combined Cadet Force of Army and Air Force with lots of mud, obstacle courses, riding, rock climbing, mountain biking, kayaking and sailing.

Summer holidays were taken with the van Straubenzees at their house near Rock in Cornwall. Healthy sea breezes were hardly the attraction. Due to the influx of the offspring of public-school teens, Rock became known as 'Sloane-Square-on-Sea' or the 'Kensington of Cornwall'. The place was awash with booze and pretty, young girls. On one occasion, Harry got drunk, throwing cider bottles. 'He was vomiting behind the wall,' said one girl. 'He's one of the most revolting people I've ever come across'.

Around his father's pad Highgrove, he also began haunting the pubs, sometimes with William and cousins Peter and Zara, who lived with Princess Anne at nearby Gatcombe Park. Sometimes there were lock-ins and Harry began to smoke Marlboro and marijuana. At Eton he soon became known as 'Hash Harry' or 'His Royal High-ness'. All these mind-altering substances were alien to the teenage Andrew, who has remained a teetotaller throughout his life, and truly unique to Harry.

Club H

Having the run of Highgrove when Charles was away, William and Harry converted the bomb-proof cellar into a club, Club H as it was known, where they hosted friends from surrounding Gloucestershire, known as the 'Glosse Posse', and threw wild parties, serving drinks from a well-stocked bar and providing around 'mind-altering substances'.

Sometimes, when fuelled with alcohol—vodka for choice—the high jinks would get the better of Harry. After drinking till 6am, he once trashed a golf course, riding around in a buggy and slashing at the grass with a golf club. And at a shooting party on the Duke of Westminster's estate a 'legless and speechless' Harry had to be put to bed while the disgruntled catering staff cleaned up after him.

Girls were involved too. Harry used the straight-forward chat-up line: 'How would you like to come back to my palace for a drink?' This sort of behaviour could not be kept from the press forever. Twenty-four-year-old model Suzannah Harvey, who stepped out with him during a hunt ball at Badminton House, later sold her story to the Sunday papers.

As the sound system in Club H could hardly be cranked up when Charles was in residence, Harry and his drinking buddies had to retreat to a local nearby. It took a relaxed approach to the licensing laws. Marijuana was smoked openly and one of the regulars was busted for selling cocaine—though it was said not to be of the highest quality. But this haven did not last long.

Harry, unlike Andrew, was rude to strangers. He got into at least one fight there and was thrown out for calling the pub's French chef a 'fucking frog', while royal protection officers looked on. But the boy had lost his mother, and no one wanted to report him to his father. However, GCHQ had been keeping his acquaintances under surveillance and MI6 leaked the information to Charles.

In a confrontation with his father, Harry confessed everything, but he thought it unfair that he was blamed when William, who he felt was equally culpable, got off scot-free. Nevertheless, Charles then got Harry to a drink-and-drug rehabilitation centre in south London that he had opened officially the previous year. The visit does not seem to have scared Harry off drink and drugs, at least according to his tell-all autobiography in which he added magic mushrooms to the list of drugs he had tried.

The story broke in the press the following January with the *News of the World* running the headline 'Harry's drug shame'. Allegations were made that Charles' spin doctors had leaked the story to portray him as a caring father. It also helped reinforce the dangers of drink and drug abuse in Harry's mind. The Queen also stepped in with the palace issuing a statement saying: 'The Queen shares the Prince of Wales's view on the seriousness of Prince Harry's behaviour and supports the action taken. She hopes the matter can now be considered as closed.' Charles also insisted that the matter had been handled within the family and was now 'past and closed'. However, at Eton it was decided not to make Harry a prefect (head boy) of his house, as William had been, because he was 'a bit of a naughty boy'.

It was around this time that Harry was getting noticed by the other sex. He lost his virginity to an older woman in a field behind a busy pub, The Vine Tree Pub in Norton, Wiltshire, who treated him 'not unlike a young stallion. Quick ride, after which she's smacked my rump and sent me off to graze.' The lady concerned, now a digger driver then a 19 year old celebrating her birthday to which she had invited the 16-year-old prince, has since broken cover to tell her story to the media.

In February 2002, Harry's great aunt Princess Margaret died. Six weeks later his great-grandmother, the Queen Mother, also passed away. Charles, William, and Harry flew back from a skiing holiday in Klosters for the funeral and moved into her former home, Clarence House, after several million pounds had been spent on refurbishment.

On his eighteenth birthday, Harry gave his first official interview. He already appeared to have mended his ways and spoke of his mother's work with AIDS charities and landmines. 'She had more guts than anyone else,' he said. 'I want to carry on the things she didn't quite finish. I've always wanted to—but before I was too young.'

He also vowed that his wild days were behind him. 'That was a mistake, and I learned my lesson,' he said. 'It was never my intention to be that way.'

He promised to devote himself to his exams at Eton, but the year ended with further tragedy when Harry's best friend Henry van Straubenzee was killed in a car accident. The two of them had planned to attend Sandhurst together. Henry and the driver, who was badly injured, were both drunk.

When Harry left Eton the following June, the press was given access to his room. Pride of place went to photographs of his mother, though there were several pin-ups including a bikini-clad Caprice—one of his Uncle Andrew's dates at the time—and Halle Berry. An eagle-eyed reporter from the *News of the World* also spotted a can of Lynx which clearly made him irresistible to his girlfriend at the time, Laura Gerard Leigh, who was a family favourite. But as his uncle experienced at this age, girlfriends were put off by the circus surrounding the spare. He consoled himself with vodka, a friend said. Next, his name was linked with a barmaid from Malmesbury.

Harry left Eton with a D in Geography and a B in Art. The latter made him look at Bristol University and consider reading art history. But he really it would have been a pretext to meet pretty girls he acknowledges. Andrew took himself a lot more serious. He had convinced himself that, following his modest princely results at Gordonstoun, a place was nonetheless waiting for him at Clare College, Cambridge, a smaller college next to his father's alma mater Trinity College. Any such hope was quickly dashed. 'We're probably among the most stringent colleges as far as academic qualifications are concerned', its admissions tutor said when asked about the prince's chances. Andrew was unphased. He opted to join the navy as a pilot straightaway. It was, he said later, a 'logical choice' as it offered the 'greatest intellectual challenge' in the military.

'I am very proud of Harry,' said a public statement issued by Charles on his son's results. 'He had worked hard for these examinations, and I am very pleased with today's results.'

Clearly, this was tongue in cheek. Harry's A-level grades were not good enough to get him a place at university, but they were good enough to get him into the royal military academy Sandhurst. However, art teacher Sarah Forsyth claimed that she had been told by a senior master to make sure Harry got a decent grade. He denied cheating and her allegations were dismissed by a tribunal, after ruling that the secret tape recordings she had made of their conversations were 'clearly an abuse of the position of trust in the pupil-teacher relationship'.

Nevertheless, the allegation earned Harry the title 'Prince Thicko' in the tabloids. It was something he would never live down. At this time in his royal the odds were well in favour of Andrew. His nickname was 'Prince Heartthrob' and, unlike rebellious Harry, he seemed well on his way to a life of luxury, footmen, being treated with kidgloves, media adulation even if he as spare never became the heir.

Spare Year

Harry took a gap year before he went to Sandhurst. During this spare year, he headed to Australia to work as a jackeroon on a remote cattle station at Tooloombilla, 370 miles from Brisbane in Queensland. It was owned by millionaire polo player Sinclair Hill and his wife Annie, who had been a friend of Diana. Seeking to evade the media, Harry made a brief photocall at Taronga Zoo in Sydney. A Palace spokesman said: 'We're concerned and disappointed that the media are not leaving him alone. He wants to learn about outback trades, not dodge the cameras.'

Naturally given his wild antics in the UK, media expectations were high that there was plenty of stroppiness to come in Australia. One newspaper reported that he 'moved with ease', throwing his arms out wide and leaping from one side to another as he jostled the cattle with a stick. He was said to be sweating but grinning and worked for about an hour at sunset.

The nearest pub, Injune Hotel, was thirty-seven miles away. The publican John McEwan complained that he had to field calls from journalists from morning to night: 'Harry's no big thing,' he said. 'We're pretty laid back out here, except for all the helicopters and the people coming in.'

Mark Dyer, who had been with Harry in Botswana, was there to shepherd the adolescent prince during his gap year and complained: 'He is in pieces. He can't do his job as a jackaroo, he can't go out, he can't even muster cattle near the road without his picture being taken.' Turning up at the local rodeo, Harry declined an invitation to ride a steer. Injune Rodeo president Jamie Johnson told ABC that Harry was 'a useless Pommy jackeroo like all of them that come out here'.

Complaints of press harassment led the Australian papers to call Harry a 'whinging Pom'. One drinker at the Injune Hotel said: 'The lad should grow up and stop whingeing. No one likes a quitter.' But the whingeing went on. It was reported that Harry and William threatened to boycott Australia in the future if he was driven out by the media. The Australian press complained in turn about the huge amount of money the government paid for his protection in the outback. The trip was not an unmitigated success.

For the second part of his gap year, Harry was sent back to Lesotho where, following in his mother's footsteps, he set up the AIDS charity Sentebale with another spare—Prince Seeiso, the younger brother of the King of Lesotho. Harry spent at least half-an-hour erecting a wire mesh fence around an orphanage compound. His photocall at the children's centre was heralded as a PR triumphs. 'I'm not going to be some person in the royal family who just finds a lame excuse to go abroad and do all sorts of sunny holidays,' he said. He made the television documentary *The Forgotten Kingdom* about Lesotho to give teeth to this assertion. Africa tends to be where the royal family goes for good PR in a nice setting. As Harry observes about Lesotho, 'Lovely country' with 'lots of need, loads of work to be done'. Even an unskilled royal can muck in with making cement and help build something somewhere.

Not everyone was impressed. The *Daily Express*'s acerbic columnist Carol Sarler called Harry 'a national disgrace' who had wasted 'the costliest education in the land' and was a 'thoroughly horrible young man' who had 'opted for eight lavish weeks in interesting parts of Africa, where he has reluctantly agreed to spend a bit of the trip staring at poor people' and 'has rarely lifted a finger unless it's to feel up a cheap tart in a nightclub or shoot some harmless critter'. The piece was headlined: 'Spoiled and lazy, Harry is one of a kind.'

Harry's communications secretary Patrick Harverson complained that Ms. Sarler's comments were a 'very unfair and unfounded attack on Prince Harry's character' which showed 'little or no understanding of Harry as a person'. Tim Luckhurst of the *Independent on Sunday* wasn't having any of it and accused Harverson of orchestrating the 'Dianification' of Harry.

Was Harry's comments about lame excuses for a sunny holiday a veiled criticism of the likes of Prince Andrew? He had had an entirely different approach to Africa as an adolescent. Andrew relished in the grovelling of former empire, now the commonwealth, and was a cheerful waver-to-the-crowds not a do-er. During the royal tour of the 'Dark Continent' he was entertained by bare-breasted dancing girls in Botswana. Harry makes no mention of this spectacle on his frequent visits to the landlocked country. In Dar-es-Salaam, Tanzania, young Andrew was even greeted by a group of British expat wives who unfurled a banner saying: 'Hi Andy, come and have coffee.' Everywhere he was in demand. Visiting Blantyre in Malawi, a man bet his wife five pounds that she would not dare ask Andrew for a dance.

'The next thing I knew I was in his arms, looking up into his eyes, such fabulous blue eyes,' she said.

After two months of leisure of work—take your pick—in Lesotho, Harry flew to Cape Town where he had a date with Chelsy Davy. When she had been at Cheltenham College, not far from Highgrove, she had become a steady member of Club H. Her mother was a former Miss 'Coca-Cola' in then Rhodesia now Zimbabwe where her father ran safaris charging up to £17,000 for a chance to shoot lions, leopards, buffalo and elephants. It was the perfect African counter part to the Beaufort Hunt and so just right for a royal. Chelsy was studying politics, philosophy and economics at Cape Town University and living with her brother in their parents' beachfront apartment in upmarket Camps Bay. She chauffeured Harry around town in her silver Mercedes.

Harry returned to England for the funeral of his grandmother, Diana's mother Frances Shand Kydd. Soon thereafter it was back to the usual: the spare going spare. There was a scuffle outside a nightclub. Photographer Chris Uncle of the Big Picture agency said: 'He burst out the car and lunged towards me as I was still taking pictures. He lashed out and then deliberately pushed my camera into my face. The base of the camera struck me and cut my bottom lip. At the same time, he was repeatedly saying "Why are you doing this? Why don't you just leave me alone?"'

The prince's protection officers pulled Harry off and pushed him back into the car. Another photographer said the prince had no reason to react as he did, adding: 'In this situation he wasn't under any threat.'

Clarence House saw things very differently. 'Prince Harry was hit in the face by a camera as photographers crowded around him as he was getting into a car,' the spokesman said.

But Harry did not mind stirring it up with the press. He once remarked: 'If I have one foot in the past and the other in tomorrow, I'm in the perfect position to piss all over today.'

Yet more princely pursuits followed. Harry flew off for the final tranche of his gap year—working on the El Remanso polo park in Argentina. Chelsy visited him there and they took off for a whirlwind weekend on a private jet, regardless of their carbon footprint. Before Christmas, he had another holiday with her with her family on Bazaruto Island, off the coast of Mozambique. No lame excuse needed.

A knee injury further delayed Harry's enrolment at Sandhurst. It meant there was now a round of parties to go to. He infamously turned up at his friend Harry Meade's 'Native and Colonial' fancy-dress party in a Nazi uniform and sporting a Hitler moustache.

'I am very sorry if I caused any offence or embarrassment to anyone. It was a poor choice of costume and I apologise,' said a statement released on his behalf. In *Spare*, he blamed William and his then new girlfriend Kate for the choice. He wasn't sure whether he should go as a Nazi or as a pilot. 'I phoned Willy and Kate, asked what they thought. Nazi uniform, they said.' He added, 'They both howled.' Still, he was the one who got into it.

Some now questioned his suitability for Sandhurst. It seemed as if he could do nothing right. For the next month, he was confined to the Duchy Home Farm, mucking out the pig stables. To keep the prince of wild fun on the rails at least until he went to Sandhurst, Charles appointed ex-SAS officer and former equerry to the Queen Mother, Jamie Lowther-Pinkerton. In a pincer move, Helen Asprey was at the same time moved in from Prince Philip's office to organise the princes' personal lives—keeping track of their polo matches and shooting parties, arranging holidays, and doing their shopping, those sorts of royal duties.

Harry and Chelsy seemed to be going steady and she flew over to London where she met Kate Middleton who, by this time, had been going out with William for two years. Chelsy's seemingly flawless integration into the family was counteracted with allegations of Harry's infidelity; Clarence House was forced to deny that Harry had cheated on Chelsy with seventeen-year-old Swedish beauty Alexia Bergstrom.

Meanwhile, Charles was preoccupied with planning his marriage to Camilla. Everyone was on their best behaviour when Charles and Camilla exchanged vows in Windsor Guildhall, though William and Harry let out a whoop.

'She's not the wicked stepmother,' said Harry. 'She's always been very close to me and William... Everyone has to understand it's very hard for her. Look at the position she is coming in to.'

Indeed, she received over 1,500 hate letters before her wedding (and, arguably, one last one belatedly in the form of *Spare*). After the wedding Harry made up with Chelsy on what the *News of the World* tastefully described as a 'sex safari' in Botswana. They camped out at the Shikawe fishing lodge and, to ensure their privacy, they hired the whole site. Nevertheless, an eyewitness said: 'Harry couldn't keep his hands off Chelsy. They also spent a lot of time snuggled up in their tent... This was their big get-together away from prying eyes and they made the most of it.' Andrew may have been lame by Harry's Africa rules, but at the same age he had seemed pompous if comparatively sane.

College Boys

Traditionally, heirs and spares are destined equally for the armed forces. Prince Andrew had already earned his wings as a glider pilot at Gordonstoun, while older brother Charles had trained on both helicopters and jet fighters. Prince Philip of course was a keen helicopter pilot and had served in the Royal Navy during World War II, earning a mention in despatches. In 1978, Charles had been appointed colonel-in-chief of the Parachute Regiment and invited Andrew to join him on a parachute jumping course. That December, Andrew went to Biggin Hill to take an aptitude test to become a pilot. The following Easter he went to RAF Benson the head-quarters of the Queen's Flight in Oxfordshire, to train on a Havilland Chipmunk.

In September 1979, Andrew followed his father and elder brother into the Royal Naval College in Dartmouth to begin a twelve-year hitch in the Royal Navy for the 'intellectual challenge' he had said he was after. His classroom attitude was the same as always, however, and his nickname among classmates was 'Golden Eagle' on account of dropping clangers when questioned by his instructors.

On his first day, he had lunch with the head of the college, Captain Nicholas Hunt, the first of many privileges other recruits resented. He had two private Gazelle helicopters for his training sessions which did little to dampen this animus among his non-royal peers.

Dartmouth was still male only, and Andrew became a little tetchy in the all male environment and short on humour that wasn't his own. 'He played the big "I am the Prince" routine all the time and seemed rather arrogant,' said one midshipman, resembling the earlier comments that were made about him by his prep schoolmates.

The wife of one of the instructors said: 'Prince Charles is still remembered with tremendous affection, but Andrew isn't popular with either the staff or his fellow cadets. His brother was a great practical joker, but Andrew walks away from anything like that. He never lets you forget who he is.'

Andrew continued to spend much of his time trying to avoid press photographers, another inevitable part of being the spare. As the only recruit allowed a car, he raced out of the gates with the paparazzi close behind in hot pursuit.

'I remember we were reversing up narrow lanes at forty miles-an-hour and doing handbrake turns around corners to shake them off,' he said. 'It was great fun, but they were very persistent.'

Sometimes their persistence paid off. One press man managed to get a picture of Andrew with naval architecture student Kirsty Robertson having a drink together in a remote pub before the landlord set the dogs on him.

After a passing-out parade attended by the Queen, Andrew was given a refresher as Charles's spare. He was given a quick course in legal and political matters in preparation should he ever become king. At the age of twenty-one, he would become a Councillor of State, allowing him to stand in for the Queen in her absence, a position from which he was sacked as King Charles's first acts as reigning monarch.

Having made headlines with his antics, Andrew made his first public speech as the guest of honour at the century dinner of the Varsity rugby match between Oxford and Cambridge. It was a boisterous affair. Fortunately, most of the audience were drunk.

When Harry finally and safely turned up Sandhurst in May 2005 he became known as Officer Cadet Wales, having at last obtained a surname of sorts. For the first five weeks, recruits are not allowed to leave the grounds. They were up before dawn, and everything done with a rigid discipline. There are no phones, no TV, no laptops, no female company, and no alcohol. Charles got an aide to tell the commandant not to spare the rod. Harry would have to polish his own boots, make his own bed with perfect hospital corners and iron his own uniform. And, for the first time in his life, he had to learn how to use a lavatory brush. His kit had to be laid out to precise formula by 5.30am.

'I was never up this early,' he told a fellow recruit, 'unless I was going to bed this late.'

Once Harry's first five weeks were over, Chelsy flew over from Cape Town to celebrate his twenty-first birthday. It was a modest affair. They had a couple of drinks in the bar at Sandhurst, but Charles gave him a £100,000 Argentinian polo pony as a birthday present. He was clearly on good terms again with his son, and it was evidently the sort of present that would always come in handy.

To mark his twenty-first birthday, Harry gave his first TV interview, telling Sky News defiantly echoing Gloria Gaynor: 'I am who I am. I'm not going to change.' Now having a mission apart from being the spare, he said he was determined to serve on the front line.

'The last thing I said was there's no way I'm going to put myself through Sandhurst and then sit on my arse back home while my boys are out fighting for their country,' he told the interviewer. 'If they said 'no, you can't do front line,' then I wouldn't drag my sorry arse through Sandhurst.' The best thing about Sandhurst, he said sounding like Diana, was 'being able to fit in as a normal person'. 'I know that I've been treated equally,' he added. 'If not in a couple of cases maybe slightly differently in the sense that "he is who he is, let's treat him even worse to make him feel really where he's at"… it did me good.'

Even sibling rivalry reared its head benignly. He said he was also looking forward to William coming to Sandhurst as his brother would have to salute him for a brief period before he leapfrogged him in rank. 'He's determined not to have to salute me,' said Harry. 'But it's the Army, isn't it?'

At twenty-one, he was also appointed Counsellor of State, ousting Prince Edward from the role. This meant that he could conduct certain functions, such as preside over Privy Council meetings, when the Queen was indisposed. He fulfilled that duty when the Queen visited Malta in November. The country, it seems, was in safe hands despite the Nazi uniform glitch. Other titles followed, another part of the job description. While still an army cadet, he was appointed commodore-in-chief in the Royal Navy. But that's the way in the royal family. A relative waves a wand and, without breaking the slightest sweat, you get to wear uniforms in branches of the service you have not served in, with a rank you have not attained, wearing medals you have not been awarded.

Prince Philip was made particularly cognisant of this. Once he was introduced to a Brazilian general who had a chest full of medals. 'What are those for?' asked Philip. The general explained that had been with the Brazilian Expeditionary Force that had fought in Italy with the Allies in World War II. 'At least I didn't get them by marrying my wife', the general added sweetly.

On 12 April 2006, the Queen, Prince Philip, Charles, and Camilla came out to Sandhurst for Harry's passing out parade. Chelsy did not attend. She was reportedly annoyed that he had celebrated the end of his military training with a visit to trashy Spearmint Rhino's lap-dancing club in Slough.

'He's let his hair down,' said a royal press secretary. "So what? Many thousands of others do the same thing".'

Was Harry finally taking his cue of Uncle Andrew, his predecessor as spare? Andrew, coming off his first tour of duty on board aircraft carrier *HMS Hermes*, had also immediately hit the headlines on shore leave in Florida after being photographed in Trader Jon's Club Pigalle in Pensacola, ogling topless go-go dancers. One of the exotic dancers, Lindy Lynn, said: 'He couldn't keep his eyes off us. Now I know where he get his "Randy Andy" nickname.' She later rechristened her performance the 'Randy Andy Eye Popper'. Like the Army, the Royal Navy weren't particularly bothered about it themselves. 'When sailors go on the town, it's only natural they want a bit of fun.' Unlike Harry, however, he wasn't in a relationship and, other than getting aroused in public, he didn't cross any lines. Another topless dancer, Sonia Larren, opined: 'He was a real prince charming. I didn't feel embarrassed at all.'

But Chelsy did show up for the ball afterwards where champagne and vodka flowed freely. There was a round of applause when the couple kissed passionately on the dance floor. It seemed that all was forgiven.

Harry joined the Blues and Royals, part of the Household Cavalry, as a second lieutenant. The regiment's colonel-in-chief was his grandmother, the Queen, while the colonel of the regiment, was his great aunt Princess Anne. It seems that having friends in high places does pay off.

On Manoeuvres

Sent on a Trooper Leaders' course at Bovington Camp in Dorset, Harry began training on tanks to become an armoured reconnaissance troop leader. However, on weekends, he would head back to London to party in exclusive bars and clubs.

It didn't look as if Harry had turned a corner. At Boujis in Kensington, he would be whisked into the VIP lounge along with William and Kate, where they would be served by their own barman. He would drink vodka and Red Bull, as well as Dom Pérignon by the magnum. Everything was served 'royal comp'. Nothing had to be paid for.

On King's Road, Harry frequented Public, a bar run by his Eton chum Guy Pelly, and the members-only nightclub Raffles. Just off Park Lane was Whisky Mist, with its low lighting and dark booths. Then round the corner was Mahiki.

'Toffs just want to have a laugh,' said Mahiki's patron Piers Adam. 'They want to take the piss out of each other. This place works because it's ironic. The bling crowd hate it. They come in and walk straight out again, because there's no smoke and mirrors, or Gucci and Prada.' Mahiki served up its signature Treasure Chest cocktail in a box. It consisted of brandy, peach liqueur, lime and sugar, topped off with Moët & Chandon and cost £100— irony didn't come cheap to the royal hangers on. At Boujis, the there was a cocktail called Crack Baby—vodka and passion fruit, topped off with champagne and served in a test tube so that you could not put it down until you finished it. History does not record its ironic price tag, however.

When it came to fashion, the princes certainly did not take after their mother. 'William and Harry's uniform comes from another age, and another cupboard,' said Peter York, author of the *Sloane Ranger Handbook*. 'It's mysterious: not speed-one hyper-Sloane, not even speed-two Johnny-Boden-Sloane. It's somewhere two rungs back from that.' This was, however, very much the royal house style. Andrew wouldn't want to be seen dead without a jacket and tie in London, at least that is what he would tell the BBC reporter on television in 2019 when interviewed about his relationship with Jeffrey Epstein.

William and Harry's phones were being hacked at the time, and his movements were reported in the papers. At least, Andrew never had to deal with this—although he had to worry about the IRA at the time which had already blown up one of his father's relatives. After closing time of his favourite clubs, Harry would go on to a private party or drink until dawn, while the royal protection squad waited outside. Often there were girls involved. News got back to Chelsy, but nevertheless, she flew over to spend the summer with him in the UK.

While other Sandhurst officers seemed star-struck around Harry, he got on particularly well with James Wharton, a soldier whom Harry saved from a beating and later came out as gay. 'The boys adored him,' said Wharton. 'They listen to him and would do anything he told them to do.' He contrasted Harry's approach to William's. 'I feel that William is already king,' Wharton said, when Prince William refused to share a joke with him.

Harry flew out to Cape Town for Chelsy's twenty-first birthday party, returning to go on manoeuvres in South Wales. Despite the military training regime in the countryside, Harry and his men managed to find a local nightclub—'the kind of place where you stick to the floor,' said Wharton. Harry prided himself that, with his men, he could go about practically unrecognised. But as Steven Wharfe always said, he resembled a labrador when it came to food. Harry blew it when he queued up for Burger King, only to realise that he was not carrying any money and one of his men had to buy a burger for him. He was still working hard at his career as the prince of fun and clueless about the workings of the real word, and despite his wish for independence, he would last long on his own, not even to buy his own burger though he would go for one if told to.

Girls, Girls, Girls

Aged 21, the two spares were running largely in tandem. Both Andrew and Harry were kept out of harm's way at Buckingham Palace with their military career. But the little time to themselves they had left, they populated as party princes surrounded by a whirlwind of women. There were differences. 'Andrew is very likeable, but he's very conscious of being a royal,' said one senior officer. He compared unfavourably with his older brother. 'You could never say that about Charles. Charles would never need encouragement to join in the fun. And he certainly wouldn't talk about girl conquests.'

All Andrew's bragging happened in private though. Unlike Harry, twenty-one-year-old Andrew was still a media darling as well as his parents' darling. America's *People* magazine put him in their list of the top ten best-looking men and he was named one of the world's most eligible bachelors alongside Warren Beatty, John Travolta, John McEnroe and Woody Allen—a curious line up under any circumstances. Attempts to deploy him as an asset for the Firm otherwise foundered nonetheless, despite the apparent sex appeal. On a trip to the US where his behaviour was so bad, he was dubbed the Duke of Yob by the British press. The American media called it 'the most unpleasant royal visit since they burned the White House in 1812'.

Back in England, twenty something Andrew's daisy-chain of relationships kept tabloid headlines busy as they would Harry's. Andrew was seen with nineteen-year-old beauty queen Carolyn Seaward, then Miss UK and runner up to Miss World. They had a candle-lit dinner together in Buckingham Palace. A footman spotted her leaving early one morning. 'Prince Andrew was very charming, witty and amusing,' she told the newspapers. 'After dinner we just relaxed, listened to music and chatted.' When asked if they had kissed, she said: 'That's question I'm not answering, but I did tell my mum afterwards.' The prince was more tight-lipped. 'We are not prepared to confirm, deny or comment on such a story,' a Palace spokesman said.

Andrew was spotted approaching a pretty blonde at Cowes. 'He really laid on the chat for a good half-an-hour,' she said. 'Then he realised I was married and toned down the yo-ho-ho stuff. He certainly likes to flirt with the girls. He knows he's good looking, but he's not conceited. He listens to what you have to say. He's interested in what you are and who you are. I suppose that's the secret of his chatting-up technique.'

He next turned up at the Ritz for Princess Margaret's fiftieth birthday party with twenty-two-year-old Gemma Curry. Her father had taught Andrew to fly at RAF Leeming. The affair foundered when he was sent to the Royal Navy air station at Culdrose in Cornwall to learn how to fly helicopters. Gemma was replaced by her cousin, twenty-two-year-old cover girl Kim Deas who dined alone with Andrew at Windsor Castle. She was also with him at his belated twenty-first birthday party at Windsor, along with Gemma and other royal favourites. DJ Kenny Everett and Elton John provided the music. Even Prime Minister Mrs Thatcher turned up to humour the Queen and see her dance with Elton John.

Whereas Harry found tabloids a nuisance, Andrew positively courted them. Kim helpfully countered comments on Andrew's behalf. He was not a male chauvinist pig after he got her to wash his car, she said after their relationship ended: 'He isn't at all. He's a lovely man. I don't want to say anything bad about him because he's still my friend. People think that because he's so good looking he's not a nice person. But he's extremely sensitive and kind. He certainly doesn't live up to his nickname of Randy Andy at all. Pressed on the details of their split-up, she said: 'I went to Buckingham Palace to see him and found him on his own watching television.' According to the aspiring model, 'He doesn't put on the prince bit at all although I'm sure he wouldn't like me to say it. He's just a very nice young man under a lot of social pressure.'

A relationship with Katie Rabett was ship-wrecked when nude pictures of her appeared in the tabloids. At twenty-three he had a brief fling with topless model Vicki Hodge when his ship, HMS *Invincible* docked in Barbados where she had a holiday home. She tried to put reporters off the scent by having him pose with her friend Tracy Lamb. In the end, she took £40,000 (around £200,000 today) from the *News of the World* for explicit details of their romps on a beach holiday they had enjoyed, including details of 'love among the scented flowers'. The story was crowned by a photograph of Andrew standing naked in the surf, swinging his swimming trunks over his head.

Vicki unkindly said she had discovered why his previous affairs had been so brief. He finished far too quickly. She took him in hand to slow things down, telling him to distract himself by counting—later complaining that he put her off by counting out loud. Nevertheless, she claimed to have converted Randy Andy from a sprinter to a marathon runner.

But, apart from the fact that there were few kiss-and-tell stories about Harry, there was, ultimately, not much daylight between the behaviour of the two spares at the same age. After three months as a jackeroo in Australia, he was spotted at the beach resort of Noosa on the Sunshine coast, going for a swim with three bodyguards and a couple of local girls, who he described as 'top totty'. He returned to Britain for Christmas, only to be snapped in the New Year in Mayfair's Chinawhite VIP nightclub kissing Page 3 girl Lauren Pope, who went on to star in *The Only Way Is Essex*. A week later, he was seen again at Chinawhite with topless model and escort Cassie Sumner. He then fell out with Annie Hall's son George, who was accompanying him on his travels, over another beauty named Ghazel Kavandi, who told the *News of the World* that she had been 'groped by Harry during a hot session of dirty dancing'. Uncle Andrew was never accused of groping though.

Into Inaction

One of the advantages—if you can call it that—of being a spare, as opposed to the heir, is that spares do get sent into combat zones. The thinking must be based on an obvious risk assessment: the heir has by now reached adulthood so if they are carefully kept out of harm's way the odds of the heir marrying and having children are pretty solid. The spare, on the other hand, is starting to look more and more supernumerary. A brave death is not unacceptable.

And so, when Argentina invaded the Falkland Islands on 2 April 1982, Andrew went to the South Atlantic with 820 Squadron on board *HMS Invincible*. But not, of course, after first hosting a squadron dinner at Buckingham Palace. The government wasn't keen and Argentina was hoping to take the prince out and it was able to sink seven ships, though not *Invincible*. In action, Andrew rescued some of the survivors from the *Atlantic Conveyor* which had been hit by an Exocet missile intended for the aircraft carrier. Andrew returned from the Falklands something of a war hero. The weather around the Falklands was atrocious and several helicopters ditched. He was awarded the South Atlantic Medal like everyone else on the campaign, but received no other special decorations for bravery. Nevertheless, he accompanied the Queen when she summoned a meeting of the editors of national newspapers in Buckingham Palace to celebrate Britain's victory.

For Harry, getting into action was not so easy. On 21 February 2007, the Ministry of Defence issued a statement which read: 'We can confirm today that Prince Harry will deploy to Iraq later this year in command of a troop from A Squadron of the Household Cavalry Regiment. While in Iraq Cornet Wales will carry out a normal troop commander's role involving leading a troop of twelve men in four Scimitar armoured reconnaissance vehicles, each with a crew of three. The decision to deploy him has been a military one. The royal household has been consulted throughout.'

Harry was delighted. But so was Abu Zaid, commander of the Malik Ibn Al Ashtar brigade of the Shi'ite Mahdi Army. He spoke about Harry with as much glee as the Argentinian junta did about Andrew, 'We are awaiting the arrival of the young, handsome, spoilt prince with bated breath and we confidently expect he will come out into the open on the battlefield. We will be generous with him. For he will return him to his grandmother [the Queen] but without ears.'

There was serious disapproval at senior levels of the military. One army officer who had completed three tours of duty in Basra told the *Guardian*: 'Wherever they place him in theatre, the concern is it will attract fire towards everyone on the ground.' Iraqi insurgents downloaded his picture from the internet and distributed them. His face is now very familiar to a lot of people—more so even than Zidane and Ronaldinho,' said Abu Samir, a leader of the Iranian-back Sunni group Thar-allah, which means 'God's revenge'. He said that they had spies planted inside the British bases to track his movements. 'As soon as the prince arrives, the race will be on to seize him as a trophy and then to decide his fate,' said another Sunni leader. Other reports came through that a team of snipers, already responsible for killing British soldiers, had been assigned to kill the prince.

At his farewell do in a London nightclub, Harry was reported as saying he was 'shitting himself'. But then the Chief of the General Staff General Sir Richard Dannatt stepped in and stopped him going. He blamed the media coverage. This delighted the critics who said that Harry had only joined the army in the first place to enhance the Windsors' glory. Even Prince Philip said he thought that Harry should never have been allowed to join the army. After all, it was the family tradition to join the navy allowing himself a little dig at his unruly grandson who had a chosen the branch of the military of his mother's friend James Hewitt. Harry himself was, reportedly, in pieces about the decision. In character of the prince of fun, he decided to get 'blotto'.

He said later that he also thought of leaving the army over it. 'It was a case of, "I very much feel like if I'm going to cause this much chaos to a lot of people then maybe I should bow out and not just for my own sake, for everyone else's sake",' he said. However, he was assured that, the next time his deployment came, there would be no prior publicity. Senior media executives agreed they would not carry stories about him heading for the combat zone, though some editors argued that this amounted to the censorship of press.

This radio silence didn't exactly solve the problem what to do with Harry.

The suggestion that he be sent to Bosnia or Africa as part of a United Nations' peace-keeping force was rejected. At a meeting chaired by General Dannatt, someone joked Harry could make a fortune as a mercenary. No one laughed. It was then decided that, if Harry was to go to a war zone, it had to be Afghanistan and he was sent to retrain as a battlefield forward air controller in Calgary.

Harry of course lapped it up in style, but also a little tone-deaf in the way of royals trapped in a royal bubble. Soon photographs of Harry canoodling with 'fake-breasted barmaids from a nightspot in Calgary' were on the front page of the *News of the World*. 'His reported question to one blonde—'are you wearing any underwear?'—sat uneasily next to news that the 150th British serviceman had just been killed in Iraq,' said the *Independent on Sunday*.

Beavis and Butt-Head

While his combat ambitions were thwarted, Harry had other concerns. The investigation into his mother's death under Sir John Stevens, Commissioner of the Metropolitan Police, had rumbled on for nearly ten years now. Over four hundred witnesses had been interviewed, including Prince Philip and Charles. The investigation concluded that Diana's death was a tragic accident. Despite the allegations of Mohamed al-Fayed, Dodi's father, there was no evidence Stevens said of a conspiracy to murder Diana, nor was she engaged to Dodi or pregnant at the time. Charles issued a statement that said: 'Prince William and Prince Harry have received a copy of the report from Lord Stevens personally. They trust that these conclusive findings will end the speculation surrounding their mother's death.'

That this was not quite an accurate statement, Harry later made clear in *Spare*. He did not fully accept the conclusion of the report. After his own extensive research—which consisted of getting his chauffeur to drive him through the Pont de l'Alma tunnel—he still thought that the paparazzi had killed his mother.

To mark the tenth anniversary of their mother's death in 2007, William and Harry gave an interview to the American network NBC's *Today Show* anchor man Matt Lauer. Asked about drinking, smoking marijuana and brawling with photographers, Harry said that, when people met him, they were surprised. 'They would say: "Oh, you're so not what I thought you were. They believed what they'd read is just poison."' Nevertheless, William stuck to his guns and said of his brother: 'Oh, he's a wild thing.'

Lauer compared them to pop stars, or talented sports stars like David Beckham.

'If you're born into it as we were,' said Harry, 'I think it is normal to feel as though you don't really want it—they choose it or they're so naturally talented at a sport they've got to deal with it.'

William said of Beckham: 'He likes selling himself, so he's fine with it.'

He wasn't looking at Harry at the time.

The interview did not go down well. It's strange how often errant royals fall into this trap. It drew criticism from an unusual source—the staunchly royalist *Daily Telegraph*. In it, columnist Jan Moir wrote: 'It's surprising how little an expensive education can do... You know what? I'm like, you know, staggered at how, duh, massively, um, inarticulate Prince William and Prince Harry are. The brothers dim went on television on both sides of the Atlantic to promote a pop concert being held to mark the tenth anniversary of their mother's death. Mistake! Especially as they sounded more like Beavis and Butthead than the privileged scions of our lovely royal family.'

She quoted Harry talking about what it was like trying to lead a normal life: 'Other people say you're not normal, so stop tryin' to be normal, which is very much what we get a lot. You know, it's like stop tryin' to be normal.'

'I see,' said Moir. 'Yes, let's stop it right there before you accidentally bite your tongue off, Prince Butthead.'

Other commentators were not so caustic. The concert at Wembley Stadium sold out. William and Harry were among the celebrity speakers at the event. A memorial service in the Guards Chapel of Wellington Barracks in Knightsbridge followed and, after a meeting with General Dannett. That was when the Queen told Harry that he was going to Afghanistan. It was considered the safer option. So, Harry was sent off to train in the Yorkshire Dales for training.

Kill TV

On 14 December 2007, wearing desert fatigues, Harry clambered aboard a C-17 Globemaster III transport plane at RAF Brize Norton in Oxfordshire for the twelve-hour flight to Afghanistan. As the plane approached Kandahar, he donned body armour and helmet. Then he flew on a CH-47 Chinook to Forward Operating Base Dwyer in the Helmand province. This was a dusty patch of ground ringed with razor wire, a ditch and machine guns which regularly came under attack.

He was housed in a rough bunker made from cages of blast-proof wire, filled with rubble. To brighten the surroundings, Harry hung a glamour-model calendar above his bunk. Otherwise, female company was at a premium. However, Harry was ribbed for chatting up Michelle Tompkins, a Harrier pilot a thousand feet over head he was supposed to be directing onto target.

His title did not come into his time in Afghanistan. He now enjoyed a new level of anonymity; he was known to the pilots he was directing only by his call sign was 'Widow Six Seven'. He spent most of his time watching monitors which showed enemy movements on what was known as 'Kill TV'.

'All my wishes have come true,' he told a reporter. 'Just walking around, some of the ANP [Afghan National Police] haven't got a clue who I am.' The Taleban, only five hundred metres away, also seemed unaware of his presence.

'It's fantastic,' Harry said. 'If I do go on patrols in amongst the locals, I will still be very wary about the fact that I need to keep my face slightly covered. Just on the off chance that I do get recognised, which will put the other guys in danger.' But he still refused to disguise his distinctive ginger locks when offered a bottle of hair dye.

The British press was told that Harry was going to Afghanistan shortly before he flew out, but they agreed to keep quiet about it in return for an interview with him by a journalist from the Press Association news agency.

A PA photographer would also be allowed to take pictures of him there.

'I honestly don't know what I miss at all,' he told them. 'Music, we've got music, we've got light, we've got food, we've got [non-alcoholic] drink.' Adding quickly: 'No, I don't miss the booze, if that's your next question.' Girls, Harry?

On Christmas Eve, Harry was transferred to the Gurkhas' Forward Operating Base Delhi in Garmsir. There Harry manned a .50 calibre machine-gun to see off Taleban patrols.

'This is the first time I've fired a .50 cal,' he admitted with a grin. 'It's just no man's land. They poke their heads up and that's it.'

He did not feel that he was in any danger there.

'When you know you are with the Gurkhas,' he said, 'I think there is no safer place to be, really.'

The conditions, again, were spartan, with no heating and little running water.

'It's bizarre,' the Prince remarked. 'I'm out here now, haven't really had a shower for four days, haven't washed my clothes for a week, and everything feels completely normal.' Harry was critical of British tactics, when ordered to withdraw. 'Harry was furious,' said Sergeant Deane Smith, 'shouting about how we'd never beat them if we didn't attack their positions and eliminate them.'

His deployment was then cut short. In January 2008, the Australian magazine *New Idea* ran the story that Harry was in Afghanistan. But no helicopter was available to pick him up. 'So, the lives of fifty soldiers were put at risk to drive Harry through areas that were littered with enemy mines,' said Sergeant Smith. Harry flew back to Brize Norton with two Royal Marine commandos who were comatose the whole way. 'One had lost two limbs—a left arm and a right leg—and another guy who was saved by his mate's body being in the way but took shrapnel to the neck,' Harry said.

Charles and William were at Brize Norton to greet Harry, where he sounded off on the media. 'I am disappointed that foreign websites have decided to run the story without consulting us,' he said, though he added that he was 'surprised by the way the British media kept to their side of the bargain.'

He also said he had achieved what he set out to do. 'As far as I'm concerned, it was mission successful because the main crux of it was to lead a troop,' he said. After all that, when he returned, he was promoted full lieutenant. After a long soak in a hot bath, he called Chelsy and was soon heading back to Botswana on three weeks leave. Harry received a service medal from Great-Aunt Anne, colonel-in-chief of the Blues and Royals, and girl friend Chelsea was present, too.

Was it all worth it though? While it may have pleased Harry and his family it is not clear that whatever Harry work did couldn't have been done with less trouble and less risk to others by someone else who did not have such a high profile.

In April 2008 the coroner's inquest into Diana's death finally came up with a verdict. The jury decided that Diana and Dodi had been unlawfully killed by the driver, Henri Paul, who was drunk. They had not been wearing seat belts. William and Harry issued a statement saying they agreed with the verdict. The coroner, Lord Justice Scott Baker, banned the jury from branding Prince Philip a murderer because there was 'not a shred of evidence' to back al-Fayed's claims that he and MI6 had conspired to kill the couple. While Harry had his doubts privately, he was not about to publicly accuse Grandpa.

While he was redeeming himself in the public's eyes with his interest in the charity for injured service personnel, Help for Heroes, and other charitable work, another pratfall from the past was to haunt him.

Three years earlier, Harry had been with other cadets waiting for a flight to Cyprus for a training exercise there. He was filming the event. As he zoomed in on the face of an Asian cadet, he said: 'Ah, our little Paki friend… Ahmed.' In the original incident was compounded when it was reported that, one night when out on an exercise, Harry said: 'F**k me! You look like a raghead.' Captain Khan said he took no offence. Nevertheless, the Ministry of Defence and the prime minister were quick to criticise. Harry was enrolled on an army diversity course to make him more racially sensitive. Perhaps we must ask Meghan whether this has worked as Harry still admits 'unconscious bias'.

At the black-tie premiere of *Quantum of Solace*, Harry still shot his mouth off and told the crowds that there was only one James Bond—and that was Sean Connery. Daniel Craig did not take offence.

'I think Prince Harry would make a fantastic James Bond,' Craig said generously about the spare. 'He's suave, and just a little bit dangerous. Like Bond, he is unpredictable and would be a perfect Bond. He's got everything it takes.' Later Harry admitted he had made a fool of himself.

Spare and Hair

Dodging controversy, Harry moved on to Middle Wallop in Hampshire, home of the Army Air Corps where he was to train as a combat pilot on the Apache attack helicopter. He said he doubted that he had the 'brain capacity' to do it, but 'I will fly what I am told to fly and whatever I am told to fly'.

Already an honorary Air Commandant in the Royal Air Force, Harry joined William at RAF Shawbury where his older brother was learning to fly fixed-wing aircraft. They shared a cottage off the base, 'for the first and last time,' Harry said. They fell out over the cooking and the tidying up. William also complained: 'He snores a lot too and keeps me up all night.' Harry groaned: 'Now they're going to think we're sharing a bed.' Still, Harry admitted that William had more brains than him, but then mentioned that his older brother was losing his hair. William retorted that was 'pretty rich coming from a ginger'.

During his stay at Shawbury, Harry made a quick visit to New York to attend a celebrity fund-raising dinner. He laid a wreath at 'ground zero'. In Harlem, he nearly gave his Secret Service body guards a heart attack, bursting children's balloons, and CBS warned of 'Harry mania'.

There were rumours that Harry was involved with singer Natalie Imbruglia after he turned up as a surgeon for her 34th birthday fancy-dress party. No armband. A guest said: 'There was no shortage of girls wanting their temperatures taken.'

However, Harry was back together again with Chelsy for this twenty-fifth birthday when he flew her and a group of friends back out to the Okavango Delta in Botswana. At twenty-five, Harry inherited £10 million from his mother's estate and the income from his part of the estate—around £6,000 a week—began flowing into his bank account, though he would not be able to get his hands on the £10 million itself until he was thirty. However, he already had £2 million that he inherited from his great grandmother, the Queen Mother, plus his salary from the Army which was around £40,000 a year. The money, he said in *Spare*, meant nothing to him. As it would probably mean a lot to a lot of people, it is not clear what point he meant to make.

More followed. His grandmother, the Queen then granted him and William their own private household with a staff of flunkies. Soon after, Harry moved in with Chelsy in her parents' £1.5-million apartment in Belgravia. He and William were pictured together in uniform in a double portrait painted by artist Nicky Philipps which was unveiled at the National Portrait Gallery. Harry complained that Philipps had made him 'more ginger than I am in real life' and that she had given William more hair. Then he was off to Barbados and South Africa on more fundraisers. But by his twenty-sixth birthday, he and Chelsy and split once more when she returned to South Africa where she intended to become a lawyer. William, on the other hand, was having more luck in that department; he got engaged to Kate Middleton.

'She's a fantastic girl,' said Harry. 'My brother's very lucky, and she's very lucky to have my brother.'

Harry then got involved in Walking With The Wounded. Four injured servicemen were aiming to walk to the North Pole to raise money for the rehabilitation of other injured service personnel. At the press launch, Harry said that he wanted to join them. Interest in the expedition rocketed and the BBC agreed to send a crew to film a documentary called *Harry's Arctic Heroes*. However, Harry would not be able to accompany them all the way. He never seemed to live up to his philanthropic aims. While the others struggled on across the snow and ice, Harry flew back to England to be William's best man and deliver the traditional embarrassing best-man speech. However, he did stay long enough in the Arctic to get frostbite on his 'todger' which has been happy enough to regale the world about it. He soothed it with the Elizabeth Arden cream that his mother used to use on her lips—which invited some Freudian interpretations.

Princely Parties

Harry spent his summer at music festivals and on a yacht with his friend Tom 'Skippy' Inskip in the Adriatic. At the open-air nightclub Veneranda on the island of Hvar off the coast of Croatia, he was bearded by local photographer Damjan Tardic.

'That was the start of an absolutely crazy night I unexpectedly spent drinking with a member of one of the most powerful monarchies in the world,' said Tardic. 'His bodyguards came up, and one of them even offered me twenty euros to back off. When Prince Harry realised I was not going to give up on him, he said to me 'Let's have a drink, and then you'll leave me alone'. He went to the bar and ordered two double vodkas and two double whiskies for the two of us. As soon as the waiter brought us the drinks, he drank it all—first the double vodka then the whisky. He immediately ordered the same again. We drank those again, in the same manner.' After that, the bodyguards asked Tardic to leave, saying: 'Now you can tell everyone you drank with the prince.' Harry then jumped in the swimming pool.

Next stop was San Diego, where he took part in Exercise Crimson Eagle, a live-fire exercise in California's Imperial Valley to acclimatize him to the dusty flying conditions he would meet in Afghanistan. Naturally, the newspapers were on the look-out for a new romance. They found it in the shape of cocktail waitress Jessica Donaldson. Apart from her elaborately tattooed midriff, she was said to have borne a striking resemblance to Kate Middleton.

After Christmas at Sandringham, Harry did not take his usual African holiday with Chelsy. Chelsy's split with Harry seemed permanent after she admitted it was not the life for her. Instead, he headed off Verbier with Beatrice, Eugenie and a number of friends. The Hotel Nevaï there was said to be home to the wildest party scene in the Alps. Afterwards he went on a hunting weekend with William on the duke of Westminster's estate in Cordoba, Spain.

By February, Harry had finished his training and was ready to go to war. But first there was more trouble to come. After spending a few days relaxing on Richard Branson's Necker Island, he headed for Las Vegas where he was seen at a pool party with Jennifer Lopez and took on the American champion swimmer Ryan Lochte in the 'twenty-metre breaststroke in jeans' race at a late-night party held at the £4,750-a-night Wynn Hotel on the Strip. Later pictures emerged of him playing strip billiards. In one shot, he protects his own modesty with his hands and a nude girl hides behind him. Another shows him bear-hugging an undressed girl with his bottom bared to the camera as they tussle with a pool cue. Buckingham Palace called lawyers in desperate attempt to prevent the embarrassing images being published in the UK or appearing on TV, though they were already widely available on the internet and in newspapers around the world. The *Sun* promptly defied the ban.

Metropolitan Police Commissioner Bernard Hogan-Howe said that his officers are not responsible for any pictures that may be taken of the prince at private functions. Harry's former chief protection officer Dai Davies said: 'His protection officers will assess the situation, and in this particular situation, other than being manhandled by women, I can't see there is an issue. From a security point of view, most of the women are naked so I couldn't see any weapons on any of them.'

Later Harry said: 'At the end of the day I probably let myself down, I let my family down, I let other people down. It was probably a classic example of me probably being too much army, and not enough prince.' Probably was an understatement.

But he said his treatment by the press over the photographs was not 'acceptable', as he was at a party where he had expected privacy. 'I don't believe there is such a thing as a private life anymore', he said, adding, 'I'm not going to sit here and whinge. Everybody knows about Twitter and the internet and stuff like that. Every single mobile phone has got a camera on it now. You can't move an inch without someone judging you, and I suppose that's just the way life goes.'

And he dismissed the press. 'No-one actually believes what they read. I certainly don't. Of course I read it. If there's a story and something's been written about me, I want to know what's being said, but all it does is just upset me and anger me that people can get away with writing the stuff they do. Not just about me, but about everything and everybody.'

It took some time for Harry to live down the strip-billiards incident. Before the WellChild awards, six-year-old leukaemia sufferer Alex Logan

Chessmen

On 7 September 2012, Harry was back in his desert fatigues again, shipping out from Brize Norton. He was heading for Camp Bastion in Helmand Province. This time the press was not informed. But just a week after Harry arrived, a Taleban attack killed two US Marines and knocked out eight Harrier jump jets. Somehow the news that Harry was there had got out. Al Jazeera reported that he was the target of the attack.

'We have informed our commanders in Helmand to do whatever they can to eliminate him,' Taleban spokesman Zabiullah Mujahid had told the press four days earlier. The date of the attack also proved significant. It was on Harry's birthday.

Harry and his four-man Apache team would be on duty twelve-hours on, twelve-hours off, awaiting orders. Their main job was to give fire support from 2,000 feet to medical teams going in to pick up injured soldiers.

'I think it's less stressful being up here than it is down there,' he said. 'We don't have to put on all the kit and walk around through the desert, sweating our balls off.'

He dismissed those who thought he had been given a cushy job because he was a royal and said that William was jealous that he got to go to Afghanistan.

'Yes, he'd get shot at but you know,' said Harry, 'if the guys who are doing the same job as us are being shot at on the ground, I don't think there's anything wrong with us being shot at as well.'

And if William got shot, Harry would move up one rung on the succession.

Life at Camp Bastion was 'as normal as it was to get', but he was irritated by the attention he got as he made his way around the base camp.

'I go into the cookhouse, and everyone has a good old gawp, and that's one thing that I dislike about being here,' he said.

On duty, he would spend most of his time in the VHR—Very High

Readiness—tent where he passed time with a PlayStation. Whoever lost the FIFA video game would be the 'brew bitch' who made the tea. Otherwise, those on call entertained themselves with board games, poker, and DVDs—which included *Apocalypse Now, Gladiator* and the *Royal Variety Performance*.

There were some royal perks though. Harry had a jar of Clarence House Garden honey, made by bees at Charles's London residence, and his father sent him a huge box of Cuban cigars, usually reserved for Jimmy Savile, which he swapped with US comrades for other treats. He also spent time communicating with Jinny Blom who was designing the 'Sentebale garden' for the Chelsea Flower Show.

When Harry returned home after his twenty-week tour of duty, he revealed that he killed Taleban insurgents. In *Spare,* Harry he claimed twenty-five, saying he thought of them merely of as 'chess pieces removed from the board'. The Apache fire controls were just like the those of the PlayStation game he had just been playing.

'We have to take a life to save a life,' said Harry. But he did not comment when NATO pulled out of Afghanistan in 2021.

To 'decompress' after the end of his second tour, Harry went skiing in Verbier with Prince Andrew, Sarah Ferguson, Beatrice, and Eugenie. He was seen cuddling Cressida Bonas, who the press was now dubbing 'the one'. Then he flew on to a fund-raiser in South Africa for the Mamohato Centre for children in Lesotho—named for Prince Seeiso's mother, Queen Mamohato Bereny Seeiso.

'I hope she would be proud of what we are trying to achieve in her name,' he said. 'I hope my mother will be proud, too. Maybe, just maybe, they are together somewhere up there, with blueprints and sketches already mapped out. I can only hope we put the swings in the right place.'

He visited the St Bernadette's Centre for the Blind and the Kananelo Centre for the Deaf where Prince Seeiso asked the children to teach Harry to sign the word for 'ginger'. Harry quickly retorted: 'What about the word for bald!'

Marriage Stakes

While Harry picked girls sensible enough to shun the limelight, Andrew went for a very different sort. After his return from the Falklands, Andrew made the headlines again with his relationship with American starlet Koo Stark who had appeared naked in movies. They had met before the war at Tramp, of all places. Andrew and his boisterous friends had been making a racket on the dance floor when she came over and asked them to turn the volume down.

'Stop being so boring,' said Andrew. 'We're having a great time, come and join us.' It was the beginning of what was said to have been his first real love affair., according to Tina Brown. He visited Koo's basement flat in Chester Square. She told her father, Hollywood producer Wilbur Stark: 'Daddy, I'm going out with a really nice guy. He's very special to me.' But she did not mention his name.

Andrew wrote to her while he was away in the Falklands. She sent pictures—one in a skin-tight outfit; another in a black T-shirt with the words 'Weird Fantasy' on the front.

Naturally, the newspapers made great play of Koo's film career, which began in 1976 with *The Awaking of Emily* where she played a seventeen-year-old who masturbates on camera. There was also a lesbian shower scene with actress Ina Skriver. Next came *Cruel Passions*, based on a story by the Marquis de Sade. She played Justine who is thrown out of an orphanage after refusing to pleasure some nuns and falls into a life of debauchery, torture, whipping, sadism, and slavery. Sodomised by Lord Carlisle, she is savaged by dogs and raped by two grave robbers. Then there was late-night TV show *The Blue Film*, which also featured explicit scenes. It was not known whether Andrew had seen any of these movies.

In 1982, Andrew invited Koo to Balmoral where she appeared in an extremely short gold ra-ra skirt. According to royal biographer Lady Colin Campbell, the Queen was 'much taken with the elegant, intelligent, and discreet Koo'. Princess Margaret lent them her holiday home, Jolies Eaux, on the Caribbean island of Mustique.

They checked into the flight to Antigua as Mr and Mrs Cambridge. By chance, *Daily Express* photographer Steve Wood was also on board. He was having a Caribbean holiday with his girlfriend Katie Hobbs. Andrew's bodyguard Geoffrey Padgham approached him and told him that he was not to take any pictures. Wood had no inkling that Andrew was on the flight and assumed that the royal passenger was Princess Margaret. Andrew disappeared onto the flight deck while Koo hid under an airline blanket. However, Katie had spotted them at the airport. So, while they were sunning themselves on Mustique, the story broke around the world. Even Koo's Spanish-born cleaning lady in London made the headlines when she told a reporter: 'I saw the *principe* leave two or three times at about nine in the morning. He always looked rather tired.'

The paparazzi hired boats to get out to the island. Local girls told reporters: 'We're all jealous of Koo... [Andrew]'s a lot better looking than Prince Charles.' And the resident steel band composed the Randy Andy Mambo in his honour.

To thwart the pressmen, the phone lines to the outside world were cut off and the island's three taxis were barred from carrying journalists. So, the paparazzi had to pursue the couple on foot while Andrew and Koo rode in a Land Rover.

Two photographers were arrested on the grounds of Princess Margaret's villa and were locked up in the island's only cell—a bare room next to the local church where they were entertained by a temperance sect singing gospel songs and served lobster provided by generous colleagues. The prince then evaded by press leaving the island by commandeering a plane hired by a photographer from the *Daily Star*, while Koo and her friends took an early morning flight to Saint Lucia, then flew to Miami where she went into hiding.

Despite the intense interest of the press, Andrew and Koo managed to spend a weekend together at Floors Castle in Scotland. She was also seen visiting his rooms in Buckingham Palace. But rumours that she would spend New Year's Eve with him at Sandringham proved false. Instead, she went skiing in St Moritz. While shopping for the trip, she was approached by a young housewife who said: 'Marry Andrew and to hell with the consequences.' Koo replied that she was in love with Andrew and Andrew loved her. But it was not to be. Others in the Palace found the relationship inappropriate, and they broke up in 1983.

The Palace were more sanguine with Sarah Ferguson—aka Fergie—the former live-in lover of racing driver Paddy McNally and daughter of Prince Charles' polo manager Major Ron Ferguson. She and Andrew had known each other as children. They met again in 1985 at a party held at Windsor Castle, during Royal Ascot week. Within a week, they had become romantically attached. It seems that Princess Diana had played matchmaker.

Andrew invited Sarah to Sandringham, the first girlfriend he had taken there since Koo Stark. His relationship with Fergie was once again hampered by his duties in the Royal Navy. But in February 1986, he was on short leave and they were staying at Floors Castle in Scotland when he dropped to his knees and said: 'Miss Ferguson, will you marry me?'

'Certainly, sir, I will,' she replied, adding: 'If you wake up and change your mind in the morning, I'll quite understand.'

By the 4th of March, Andrew was back in his quarters in Buckingham Palace when he called Garrard, the royal jewellers, and asked them to bring a selection of suitable engagement rings. Although Fergie found several she liked, he was not satisfied and produced drawings of what he wanted. The workshops at Garrard then set about making an eighteen-carat white and gold ring with a Burma ruby surrounded by ten drop-diamonds. It was ready in a week. She wore it for the first time on the 17th of March, the day the engagement was announced.

On March 15th, they had been to Windsor to see the Queen. When they got her permission to marry, they toasted the occasion with champagne. When she went back to her job at a publishing house the following Monday, she was accompanied by two uniformed policemen and two plain-clothed officers to see her through the press cordon outside her office.

They did a television interview sitting side by side in Andrew's study where she showed off the ring.

'It had to be something red,' said Fergie, being a red head. 'I wanted a ruby—well, I didn't want a ruby, I'm very lucky to have it.'

'We came to the conclusion that red was probably the best colour for Sarah,' Andrew chipped in. Afterward they kissed on the back lawn of the Palace for the photographers.

They were to be married by the Archbishop of Canterbury in Westminster Abbey on 23 July. Unfortunately, his ship HMS *Brazen* would be in the Middle East then and his fellow officers would not be able to form a guard of honour. He would also be stood down from his duties as a helicopter pilot on HMS *Brazen* and sent to Greenwich Royal Naval College to study economics and defence policy in preparation for a promotion.

Andy and Fergie loved appearing on TV. It was a medium where they thought they could do no wrong. Little did they know. She was also shown displaying her new wardrobe and she shrugged off criticism of her fuller figure.

As Andrew was a spare, their wedding day was not to be a public holiday, unlike Charles and Diana's. But security was tight with the SAS on the rooftops and armed detectives dressed as coachmen riding on the back of the carriages. Five miles of sewers under Westminster had been checked.

At 10am, an announcement was posted on the railings of Buckingham Park saying that the Queen had conferred on Andrew the titles Duke of York, Earl of Inverness, and Baron Killyleagh—one English title, one Scottish, and one Irish. She loved conferring titles on the family. To mark death of the Queen Mother in 2002, it was suggested that Prince Philip become a Knight of the Royal Victoria Order. Philip rejected the offer saying it was 'an order for servants'. But in a private ceremony at Buckingham Palace in 2011, the Queen made Andrew a Knight of the Grand Cross of the Royal Victorian Order before the two of them settled down for tea.

Fergie arrived at Westminster Abbey in a gold coach. She wore a dress adorned with silk flowers. Heavy beadworks incorporated various symbols including hearts representing romance, anchors and waves representing Prince Andrew's navy background, and bumblebees and thistles, which were taken from Sarah Ferguson's dubious family heraldry. Ever tasteful it had a seventeen-foot train with the initials A and S intertwined in silver beads. The bodice was boned to give her a slim waist. She said she lost twenty-six pounds to fit into it.

Some 1,800 guests, including a who's who of celebs, awaited at Westminster Abbey. She arrived in an 1881 Glass Coach. The trumpeters of the Royal Marines sounded a fanfare and the organist struck up Edward Elgar's 'Imperial March'.

'More carriages, more pomp,' she said. 'Wonderful, I love it.'

Afterwards there was a traditional wedding breakfast for 120 guests at Buckingham Palace. The newlyweds and some three hundred guests moved to a party at Claridge's hotel. They set off for Heathrow Airport in an open carriage. The royal jet then flew them to the Azores where they spent their five-day honeymoon on board the royal yacht *Britannia*.

Their marriage was passionate at first and their very public displays of affection sometimes embarrassed friends. On one occasion, the Prince even interrupted a naval exercise so that he could spend two hours with her in a cabin on a support ship. This was not a privilege extended to other sailors. The excuse: seasickness.

Toe Curling

Fergie soon grew tired of her marriage to Andrew. He was always away on duty. In 1990, she complained that they had only spent forty-two nights together during their four years of marriage. To make matters worse, when he was home, he devoted most of his energies to playing golf. Meanwhile she put on weight, leading the press to dub her the Duchess of Pork. Ever resourceful, she later capitalized on the name by becoming the US spokesman for Weight Watchers International.

Bored, Fergie began gallivanting round London clubs with the newly liberated Princess Di and jetting off on endless holidays at the taxpayers' expense. She also shredded all Prince Andrew's love-letters on the pretext that they might be stolen. She was criticized for having to too many holidays and accepting too many free gifts, earning her the nickname 'Freeloading Fergie'. In response, she complained that her allowance would not cover first-class air travel. She demanded payment for interviews and asked designers to give her free clothes. Furthermore, she only made 108 official engagements in 1991, compared to Princess Anne's 768.

Some embarrassing pictures of her father, Major Ronald Ferguson at the Wigmore Club, a London massage parlour where sexual services were provided, found their way into the press. Then in January 1992, 120 photographs were found by a cleaner in the London flat of Texan playboy Steve Wyatt. They showed the American and Fergie holidaying together. This led Andrew to ask for a divorce and turn for succour to former lover Koo Stark. Another old flame, thirty-eight-year-old divorcée Jane Roxburghe, also provided a shoulder for him to cry on.

The Queen ordered Fergie to stop seeing Wyatt, but the newspapers reported that she secretly visited his flat on at least two more occasions. The announcement that the Yorks had separated was made on 19 March 1992.

To escape from the growing scandal, Fergie headed out to Florida where she stayed with sixty-six-year-old Robert Forman, who prided himself on his boast of going out with girls young enough to be his granddaughters. Was he Andrew II in the making?

Then she went for a holiday in the Far East with her financial adviser Johnny Bryan, who was later photographed sucking the toes of a topless Fergie. The divorce was finalized in 1996, allowing Andrew the chance to go back to his old ways.

Although divorced, Andrew and Fergie continued to live in Sunninghill Park, the two-storey red fifty-room brick mansion built by the Yorks in Berkshire with a staff of eleven. It was mocked as 'Southyork' after 'Southfork', the Texan oil tycoon's estate in the 1980s soap opera *Dallas*. The estate had been given to the couple as a wedding present by the Queen and the couple expected equipment suppliers to furnish the kitchen and bathroom free of charge. Notable was a giant marble bathtub that the builders dubbed HMS *Fergie*.

Andrew lived there until 2004, when he moved into Royal Lodge in Windsor. Fergie moved out in 2006. She rented Dolphin House, just next door to the Royal Lodge. The following year, there was a fire at Dolphin House and Fergie moved into Royal Lodge with her former husband. Despite being divorced, they seemed to have no issue continuing to live together.

After several years on the market, Sunninghill Park was sold in 2011 for £15 million—£3 million over the asking price—to Kazakh oligarch Timur Kalobeyei, though by then it was almost derelict. He had it knocked down. Kulibayev was the son-in-law of the president of Kazakhstan Nursultan Nazarbayev who Andrew had met as UK trade envoy. The deal attracted the interest of prosecutors in Italy and Switzerland.

'We cannot be clearer that there is no question of the Duke of York having benefited from his position as special representative in his sale of the property,' the prince's spokesman said. 'Any suggestion that he has abused his public position is completely untrue. The sale was a straight commercial transaction.' As always Buckingham Palace also rallied to the defence of the beleaguered prince, issuing a statement saying: 'There was never any impropriety on the part of the Duke of York, any suggestions of which are false.'

The Royal Lovable Rogue

The problem of being a spare is that you have no real role and, in the case of Andrew, no income except for what the monarch may give you. The heir at least can be seen to be in training to take over the reins, but as the spare inevitably slips down the lineage. Prince Harry sought to fill his time with charity work as he had no money worries. This brought him into conflict with big brother Willy and the two of them, like nineteenth-century colonists, fought over who should do their bit for Africa. However, there was still one area that Harry could trump William. He had seen front-line fighting; William had not. And he had been involved in Walking With The Wounded. According to Harry, William said: 'I let you have the veterans, why can't you let me have African elephants and rhinos?'

When it appeared that Africa was not big enough for both of them, Harry flew by private jet to Warrior Games for disabled service personnel in Colorado Springs where he proposed holding a similar event in the UK. Every tactful, he told his American audience: 'I hope this is something you will all take a huge interest in as your nation will be coming probably second if not third to the UK team.'

Two days after the birth of Prince George, who bumped him down the succession to fourth in line to the throne, Harry attended the Sentebale's Stories of Hope exhibition at the Getty Images Gallery. It was a showcase for the work of the charity and Harry's part in it. The following month he travelled to Angola to continue his mother's work with the Halo Trust, set up in 1988 to help clear landmines.

The trust's chief executive Guy Willoughby said: 'He is irritated about the countries that supplied these landmines are not actually putting in any funds to clear them twenty-five years later. He has got quite a bee in his bonnet about that.' Willoughby fell from grace and was suspended by the charity.

That October, Harry visited Australia where he spoke in front of an audience that included disabled Australian war veterans and Paralympians.

Prime Minister Tony Abbott responded, saying: 'Prince Harry, I regret to say not every Australian is a monarchist.' His twenty-year-old daughter needed no convincing. She posted a picture of her and Harry, and tweeted: 'He's the perfect Prince Charming. I'm single and, well, he's the prince.'

Meanwhile his relationship with Cressida Bonas was blowing hot and cold. The 'party prince' was now keen to marry and settle down, but Cressida thought she was too young. After attending a James Blunt concert, they split up for a month while Harry trekked to the South Pole for Walking With The Wounded—a brave move given the todger damage he'd sustained on his last polar expedition. This time he needed urgent medical attention after suffering severe altitude sickness, exhaustion, and dehydration. In the documentary *Harry's South Pole Heroes*, he said: 'Antarctica jumped up and bit me on the arse.'

In January 2014, he quit his role as an Apache helicopter pilot and took a desk job. He left Kensington Palace to William and Kate and moved into Nottingham Cottage. After being dumped by Cressida, Harry went to Memphis, Tennessee for the wedding of Guy Pelly and Holiday Inn heiress Lizzy Wilson. He took with him an Elvis-sized entourage. There was Thomas van Straubenzee and Tom 'Skippy' Inskip who had been with Harry on the ill-fated trip to Las Vegas, the bash on the Croatian Island of Hvar and a party in 2010 when Harry had inhaled nitrous oxide. Also on hand were Harry Meade, whose party Harry had turned up to in his Nazi uniform, polo player and Ralph Lauren model Nacho Figueras, Luke and Mark Tomlinson from the Beaufort Polo Club and rugby player James Haskell. Charming company.

Harry's close friend, soul singer Joss Stone, sympathized with his struggle to find love as he approached thirty. But it wasn't long before Harry was 'spotting snogging with a mystery brunette' at Guy Pelly's Sloane Square tequila club Tonteria. This turned out to be twenty-five-year-old Camilla Thurlow, who the press dubbed 'Cressida 2.0'. An alumnus of Fettes College, she represented Edinburgh at the finals of Miss Earth UK, an eco-friendly beauty pageant in 2008, and played in the Scottish team at the World Lacrosse Championship in Canada in 2007. Jolly hockey sticks.

In March 2014, Harry launched the Invictus Games, funded by £1million of bankers' Libor fines, matched by £1 million from the Royal Foundation, a charity originally set up with brother William. The first games took place in London that September. The Invictus Games marked a high point in Prince Harry's royal career. It allowed him to play the role of compassionate carer that his mother had perfected by giving voice to an underrepresented group.

In January 2015, Kensington Palace also announced that he would be leaving the army later that year, after a stint in Australia. Harry complained to friends that he was under pressure to carry out more official engagements. In all, he had attended 94 engagements in 2014—hardly a burden compare to the 533 his father did. Even the pregnant Duchess of Cambridge did 91, despite suffering from morning sickness.

It is not always clear what counts as an official engagement. Harry did find time to turn out for the World's Darts Championship as a guest of the sponsors at Alexandra Palace, where he reportedly enjoyed 'champagne-fuelled aristocratic banter' in the VIP suite. He also squeezed in a little polo at Cirencester Park Polo Club in Gloucestershire.

The *Daily Telegraph* reported that Prince Harry had 'become the nation's favourite lovable rogue'. Meanwhile Playwright Jon Conway, author of the play *Truth, Lies, Diana* said that Hewitt had told him, in a 'startling revelation', that his 'relationship with Diana started eighteen months before Prince Harry was born'. In the play, the character who plays Hewitt says: 'Diana and I started our relationship more than a year before Harry was born. Now that does not prove that I am his father. It's just the... inconvenient truth.'

Former Tory MP and *Strictly Come Dancing* contestant Ann Widdecombe condemned the speculation about Harry's paternity as 'tasteless and hurtful, but also daft'. The family rallied round.

Meanwhile his recent ex-girlfriend, Cressida Bonas, was making waves of her own. She went skiing with Princess Eugenie and Prince Andrew, who was beginning to become embroiled in the Jeffrey Epstein scandal and was cast by in the movie *Tulip Fever* by Harvey Weinstein who would soon have problems of his own.

After returning from the £22,000-a-week chalet where Andrew was besieged by the world's media over allegations that disgraced financier Jeffery Epstein had procured an under-age girl to have sex with him, something Andrew has strenously denied, Cressida posed in a mid-riff-baring outfit with Weinstein at the premier of his latest film *Big Eyes*. The *Daily Mail* noted that Weinstein was 'known for mentoring young actresses'.

Unencumbered Harry was seen out on the pull at Bodo's Schloss, an après-ski-themed bar in High Street Kensington which boasted waiters wearing lederhosen, £1,000 sharing cocktails and a discrete back entrance for the younger royals. A little more down-market, he also favoured the Nando's in Fulham and the Brown Cow pub nearby. But his favourite nightclub was still Boujis in South Kensington, which was being investigated by the licensing authority after complaints about vomiting, urinating, and fighting in the street outside. The police had been called thirty-two times in a year over incidents of theft, public order offences and 'failure to comply with door staff'. Later there were problems at Bodo's Schloss too, following a glassing incident involving a relative of Formula 1 mogul Bernie Ecclestone that left two men in hospital. Perhaps seeking the safety of London's East End, it was reported that Harry had sought sanctuary in a warehouse rave in Bethnal Green Road.

Nor did Harry's duties in the Army prevent him joining the royal skiing party at Uncle Andrew's pricey chalet in Verbier, bought with the help of the Bank of Mum. Nor could he resist downing a few rum cocktails and smoking a shisha pipe at a pop-up nightclub on board a yacht in the Gulf during the Abu Dhabi Grand Prix.

Nevertheless, he came eighth in a YouGov survey of the UK's most respected men, behind Stephen Hawking, David Attenborough, Barack Obama, Richard Branson, his brother Prince William, the Dalai Lama and Bill Gates, and above both the Pope and David Beckham. Another survey for the *Daily Mail* found William and Harry were the most popular members of the royal family, with Andrew languishing at the bottom of the poll. The *Mail* also revealed that Harry had inhaled the recreational drug nitrous oxide. He was laughing; he managed to keep his public reputation intact even after all his antics.

Big Game Hunting

In March 2015, Kensington Palace issued a statement confirming that Prince Harry would be leaving the Army after a four-week secondment to the Australian Defence Force, starting in April. It was 'a really tough decision,' he said. 'I consider myself incredibly lucky to have had the chance to do some very challenging jobs and have met many fantastic people in the process.'

Harry said he planned to spend time in Africa, pursuing his interest in conservation and wildlife in yet another gap year at the age of thirty, without. Coincidentally, Nick House, the owner of Bodo's Schloss as well as the clubs Mahiki and Whisky Mist, was also heading for Africa, aiming to open a club named Carbon in Accra, the capital of Ghana. The public seemed to enjoy having him around as the prince of fun so why not make the most of it?

Arriving in Canberra, he was greeted with a banner that said: 'Redheads rule.' Brother William called him 'Big Ginger'. Harry then larked around and high-fived other carrot-tops, but refused to take a selfie with a girl, insisting that she take a 'normal photograph' instead. 'Selfies are bad,' he declared.

'Normal photographs' were also taken later showing Harry toting a Steyr assault rifle while on manoeuvres with Royal Australian Artillery troops near Darwin in the Northern Territory. Soon after, Harry was with his father greeting relatives of veterans of the Gallipoli campaign on the flight deck of HMS *Bulwark* in the Dardanelles marking the hundredth anniversary of the first day of the landings. He wore the white dress uniform of the Household Cavalry while Charles wore full naval dress.

Harry then paid a flying visit to London to present a lifetime achievement award to long-distance runner Paula Radcliffe before jetting back to Australia for anti-terrorism exercise with the Royal Australian Navy and the Aussie SAS. Meanwhile, he was bumped down to fifth in line to the throne by the birth of Princess Charlotte, another spare.

This did not sit well with fellow redhead and wannabe terrorist Mark Colborne. The Old Bailey was told that he had planned to assassinate Prince Charles and Prince William so Harry could be king. Colborne was detained indefinitely under the Mental Health Act.

Consolation was offered to Harry by Chelsy Davy who reportedly sought to rekindle their romance. She had some competition though. When Harry bid farewell to Australia from the Sydney Opera House, hundreds of screaming girls turned out with banners reading: 'Marry Me, Harry', 'His Royal Hotness' and 'Red Heads Rule'. Twenty-one-year-old Victoria McRae stole a kiss while making her third proposal of marriage to the royal visitor. It was his final chance, she said. He promised to think about it. In New Zealand, he was greeted by more female fans carrying homemade placards. One girl, wearing traditional Maori dress, performed the ancient 'hongi' greeting, pressing her forehead and nose against his while exhaling heavily, apparently imparting the 'breath of life'. It was eerily similar to the time Andrew was travelling to the former colonies.

Back home in London French actress Camille Cottin, aka *La Connasse* (The Bitch), was awaiting his return. She spent ten minutes outside Kensington Palace crying 'Harry, Harry' before trying to scale the gates in high heels. After being led away by the police, she explained that she was seeking the hand of 'the last bachelor prince who is not deformed (even if he is a redhead)'. The incident was filmed for the movie *Connasse: Princesse des coeurs*, (*Bitch: Princess of Hearts*). It was released in cinemas in France and made $8.3 million at the box office.

Ruing his misspent youth, Harry called for the return of National Service, saying his time in the Army had straightened him out. Had it though? Then he said he planned to spend more time gardening while showing the Queen around his Sentebale African charity's show garden at the Chelsea Flower Show. Instead, he returned to the polo field and was seen hanging out with Hollywood star Samuel L. Jackson at the annual polo tournament sponsored by Audi at Coworth Park in Berkshire. A champagne-fuelled Harry was later seen taking to the dance floor. A lot of actresses were actively courted and society pages filled with photographs.

On 4 June 2015, the Queen made Harry a Knight Commander of the Royal Victorian Order for 'services to the sovereign' as 'a sign of his grandmother's personal esteem for him and his growing status in the family after he decided to leave the Army'. Courtiers were surprised that he was only made a Knight Commander (KCVO) not a top-notch Knight Grand Cross (GCVO) of the order. Sophie Wessex, Camilla and most of the

Queen's chamberlains, secretaries and officers get the GCVO.

'It's a shame,' said a palace insider. 'Harry might like the GCVO's red, white and blue sash. It's known as the Miss UK because it's worn in the style of a beauty queen.'

Harry cost the taxpayer £100,000 using a private jet as the best way to travel around Brazil during the World Cup. His name was linked with that of twenty-nine-year-old socialite Antonia Packard whose mother was Brazilian beauty Dulce Maria de Barros Marchi. For Antonia this seems to have been a dream come true. On her Facebook page, she is seen kissing a frog. Kensington Palace took the highly unusual step of formally denying the story.

In Namibia, Harry tranquilised a rhino with a dart-gun. He deftly chain-sawed off a large chunk of horn without damaging vital tissue and drew blood for DNA sampling. Namibia's Minister of Environment and Tourism, Pohamba Shifeta, warned against the royal trip turning into a publicity stunt. He had not even been aware that Harry was planning a visit until two weeks earlier. 'Harry is not the first prominent person to visit Namibia,' Shifeta said, 'but we don't want it to turn into a public relations exercise.'

Government official, Colgar Sikopo, who was instructed to find out where Harry was and what he was doing, added: 'We have a model system here with which we are gradually defeating poachers. We cannot have foreigners—even if they are members of the Royal Family—turning up here and announcing they are going to get involved.'

In Botswana he was photographed petting a tranquillised lion. He was accompanied by two royal protection officers and told Simson Uri-Khob, boss of charity Save The Rhino: 'I have even more bodyguards at home, it's worse than here. There are more of them, they're everywhere.'

Simson said: 'We asked him what about if you're with a girlfriend. Are they around then? Harry said, "Unfortunately yes, more than ever. But I know how to handle that."' How was obviously the next question, but history remains silent on this point. Meanwhile, another essential part of the job description of being a spare came to the fore—be subjected to speculation who the prince might choose as his princess? Never mind that everything Harry did (like Andrew at the same age) showed he was a professional Prince of Fun and made abundantly clear any which way that marriage was the last thing on his mind.

Ginger Nuts

During his field trip in South Africa, Harry roughed it at the £250-per-night luxury Bush Lodge, which includes those safari essentials—a TV, en-suite bathroom, and kitchen. It also offers the option of a personal cook and wildlife guide. The *Daily Mail* also reported a secret tryst with Chelsy Davy in the African jungle, prompting speculation that the two were getting back together again. Other newspapers reported that she had given him a special birthday present after they bumped into each other accidentally-on-purpose, holidaying in her native Zimbabwe.

Back in England, Chelsy helped Guy Pelly organize a combined welcome-home party and birthday bash for Harry—a booze-fuelled cruise on the Thames with his closest friends. Still, according to the papers, he was a man looking to get married. 'Harry still holds a candle for her,' a source told the *Daily Mail*. 'Chelsy has his heart. They saw each other recently. There's still very much something between them, but Chelsy won't commit yet because she doesn't want to lead a life in the spotlight. Harry's very sensitive to that. He has never fallen out of love with Chelsy.' The following day, the *Mail* reported that Harry had spent his birthday with Cressida in The Cross Keys, a pub in Chelsea. He was seen smoking a cigarette—a habit he had picked up at Eton—outside and he left the venue at 1.30am with another blonde woman. Anything but marriage was on his princely mind.

The big news, however, was that he was sporting a beard. The newly hirsute Harry had set Twitter, well, twittering. One tweet said he looked 'hotter than ever'. 'Yum, yum,' said another, 'you sexy thing.' A third said: 'I'd like to thank not only Jesus but God herself for blessing us with Prince Harry's beard.' By then Harry's beard had its own Twitter account where a spoof tweet appeared saying: 'One at a time, ladies, I can't handle all this attention. There's only one of me.' *Vanity Fair* note that the royal growth was 'more vibrant, more lush, than ever before', while in the *Daily Mail* columnist Hannah Betts' reaction risked cardiac arrest.

'I must confess, I have long carried a torch for the House of Windsor's resident ginger nut: a man who is witty, brave, self-deprecating, genuinely does things, and serves as a charming and relaxed ambassador for our country. There is also the small matter that he is as hot as Hades,' she wrote. 'However, the beard has pushed the ardency of my crush seriously off the scale, propelling me into a whole new level of middle-aged, yet curiously girlish, adoration.'

The Rugby World Cup revealed the first sign of a falling out between the two brothers. Harry was England rugby's honorary president, while William was vice-patron of the Welsh Rugby Union.

Promoting her autobiography *Storm in a C Cup*, *X-Factor* presenter Caroline Flack complained that her family had been hounded following rumours that she was dating Prince Harry. Not to be outdone, *Britain's Got Talent* judge Alesha Dixon said she had been chatted up by Harry in a nightclub. In America, *OK!* magazine added that Harry had pursued Pippa Middleton after Kate caught them snogging in the bathroom at the royal wedding. Pippa broke off the romance for fear of upsetting her sister.

But help was at hand. The *Daily Mail* reported that Camilla was busy hunting for a wife for Harry. Columnist Amanda Platell suggested Kirstie Ennis, a US marine veteran helicopter gunner who carried out thirty-eight operations in Afghanistan, almost died in a crash that cost her a leg and had just completed a 1,000-mile walk in the UK to raise money for Harry's charity. She and the Prince were pictured embracing after her epic achievement and are said to have struck up a close bond. 'So, forget the endless list of airhead floozies,' said Platell. 'It would do Harry and his family a power of good if he married someone like this remarkable young woman.'

The *Mail on Sunday* revealed that Harry has been in daily contact with the twenty-four-year-old since the operation that removed her lower left leg. They had met at the Warrior Games in Colorado in 2013. She had posted a picture of herself posing seductively in a red bikini before the amputation. 'I wanted to show how I looked before surgery,' she said. 'I wanted to show that with or without my leg, I am still beautiful.' Harry was said to be completely in awe of Kirstie and was looking forward to seeing her at the Invictus Games in Orlando in May.

While Kristie was indebted to Afghanistan, Harry spent his time in Africa. He opened a £2-million care home for children affected by HIV and Aids in Lesotho, continuing his mother's legacy. He named its welcome centre after Olga Powell, his former nanny who had been charged by Princess Diana to give William and Harry a 'normal' upbringing and make them at ease in the real world.

In recognition of his charity work in southern Africa, Desmond Tutu awarded Harry the Order of the Companion of Honour in Cape Town. Afterwards he kicked off his trainers to play a game of touch rugby with gang members at a correction centre in the townships, where he told the teenagers: 'I didn't enjoy school at all. I would like to have come to a place like this. When I was at school, I wanted to be the bad boy.' Perhaps spare princes should be seen and not heard.

Columnist Sarah Vine jeered: 'Come on, Harry—swap life as fifth in line to the British throne for a dirt-poor upbringing in the townships of South Africa? You're insulting our intelligence.'

Amanda Platell pitched in: 'Currently out in Africa hugging elephants, Prince Harry ponders his importance as a role model: 'We have a certain responsibility to make sure young people look at us and say: 'That's how I want to live.'' What? Still living at home in his 30s, unemployed and financially dependent on his father? Hardly a perfect role model for today's youth.'

Flights alone on the South Africa trip cost £25,936. Columnist Rachel Johnson sniped: 'How long is his endless gap year going to last?' The visit cost £33,278, total though this was frugal by the standards of his uncle 'Air-miles Andy'.

Back in Britain, Harry's approval rating hit 70%, outstripping even that of the Queen. The *Daily Mail* said: 'William will be King, but Harry will be People's King—that's the plan.'

Journalist Rachel Johnson stated that 'we all secretly long for' Harry to be King. Harry inherited his grandfather's outspokenness, lambasting the rise of the social media while using it to promote his Invictus Games. Meanwhile he bemoaned his situation. 'I thought long and hard about getting a job,' he said. 'I don't get any satisfaction from sitting at home on my arse—and that's a body part, by the way, not a swearword.'

The *Mail* was still trying to marry him off and linked him to twenty-four-year-old actress and model Suki Waterhouse.

'She's a young, blonde socialite who loves dancing and has a good sense of humour. And she's single. So far, so Prince Harry's type,' the *Mail* said while speculating that Harry had been put off the idea of marriage by his parents' acrimonious divorce. He was seen with Suki at a party she hosted in Notting Hill sponsored by vodka brand Ciroc. Also on hand were a bevy of other blondes—actress Sienna Miller, supermodel Cara Delevingne, Australian actress Margot Robbie, TV presenter Poppy Jamie and Harry's cousin, Princess Eugenie.

Reporting on the party, the *Mail* hedged its bets also putting forward the name of twenty-two-year-old American fashion PR Juliette Labelle who he had met in LA over the New Year. The race was on as the bachelor chums, with whom he used to fool around, were all getting married. By the end of the month, the newspaper reported that he was 'rather smitten' by twenty-nine-year-old actress Jenna Coleman, though she was thought to be dating *Game Of Thrones*' star Richard Madden.

In a series of interviews, Harry complained about incessant intrusions into his private life,. He also voiced his fears of being overshadowed by Prince George as the nephew who took his number three spot in the succession grew up. But it was noted how well he got on with his sister-in-law Kate. While some accused him of flirting with her, it was said she was like the big sister he never had.

Business As Usual

While Harry thought about getting a job, it was not for everyone. Andrew ended his naval career in 2001 with a spell at the Ministry of Defence but found the work there a strain.

'It got a little bit wearing at times,' he said. 'It became very evident in the summer of last year that I was doing too much. I was feeling tired. No, no, no, it was just doing little things, you're not always on peak performance. But that's the way the cookie crumbles and you just get on with it.'

No one knew yet that, a decade later, another cookie would crumble and that Virginia Giuffre would accuse him of sexual assault on three occasions in March 2001 against strenuous denials from the prince who denied ever meeting her.

But that was the future. When Andrew came off the active list in the summer of 2001 he still managed to get promoted afterwards as is the royal family's wont. Three years later, Commander York was made an honorary captain though he had quit the navy. On his fiftieth birthday in 2010, he was promoted honorary rear admiral and made an honorary vice admiral five years later. He was also appointed the UK's Special Representative for International Trade and Investment. This position was unpaid but offered plenty of opportunities for lucrative side-lines. Otherwise, he would have had to live on the £249,000 a year his mother gave him and the £20,000-a-year pension he got from the Navy.

When in Britain Andrew still lived with Fergie and his daughters. On his fortieth birthday they caused outrage when they pulled up at the Millennium Wheel in their official Jag and jumped the queue forcing others to wait in the cold for an extra hour.

'I can't believe they have made us all wait this long just so Andy and Fergie could get a free ride,' said one man in the queue. Another would-be rider shouted: 'You lot are nothing but freeloaders.'

Despite the boos, they smiled and waved at the crowd.

Five of Andrew's former girlfriends turned out for the birthday party Fergie put on for him. Caprice could not make it that day, so Andrew later prevailed on the staff at St. James's Palace to let him have a suite of state apartments for the night and to lay on a lavish dinner for the former *Playboy* model. The table was decked with elaborate candlesticks, flowers, silver cutlery and China with the royal crest and the meal was served by liveried footmen. However, his name was soon linked to that of twenty-three-year-old French professional golfer Audrey Raimbault, who he sneaked into Buckingham Palace for a tour of his private quarters. She also stayed at Windsor on at least two occasions.

And there was continued talk that Andrew and Fergie would remarry. The couple had recently been on a holiday with daughters Beatrice and Eugenie in the Bahamas.

In an interview in *Tatler* magazine in June 2000, he said: 'I don't rule remarriage out.' Fergie added: 'I simply say, if it should happen, great. It is not in, nor is it ruled out.' In a rare moment of introspection the prince also admitted that he knew he had a reputation as a 'cack-handed, blonde dating oaf '. The prince was 'sensitive to the nuances of the way he has been portrayed'. He blamed himself for missing 'the cries for help' from Fergie until it was too late to save the marriage.

But Andrew was by now an experienced hand. He knew that his job was to fan the marriage speculation game rather than resist it. That didn't mean he had to take it very seriously. Before Fergie's interview could even be published, he was seen out with supermodel Christy Turlington. Then there was model turned TV presenter Catrina Skepper, PR executive Aurelia Cecil, South African waitress turned model Heather Mann who was invited to the Queen Mother's hundredth birthday party at Windsor, former Miss USA Julie Hayek who he dined with *à deux* in Manhattan and former *Playboy* model Denise Martell. Even American rock star Courtney Love claimed that Andrew came knocking at her door at one in the morning 'looking for chicks'.

Actor George Hamilton introduced Andrew to his former daughter-in-law Angie Everhart who had appeared in several *Sports Illustrated* swimsuit issues and posed nude for *Playboy*. 'George told me, 'He likes redheads, and he has a wish list of girls he'd like to meet while he's in town—and you're on it',' she said. The attraction, apparently, was that she was a redhead like Fergie, not Harry.

Angie took the possibility of becoming the next duchess of York seriously, according to the press at any rate. 'I'd have been a bit more popular than the last American, that Duchess of Windsor,' she told the *Mail on Sunday*.

Andrew's name was also linked with billionaire Kazakh socialite Goga Ashkenazi. Royal watcher Margaret Holder said: 'The playboy image is not one Prince Andrew discourages. He's been seen many times on these party yachts, and he thinks it enhances his reputation. Attracting luscious young ladies makes him feel young.' By 2010, she reckoned he had been through about fifteen girlfriends since his divorce.

It was even suggested that Fergie was a matchmaker introducing Andrew to some non-threatening girls. In 1998, when Andrew's relationship with Aurelia Cecil was supposedly getting serious, it was Fergie who was thought to intervene by introducing him to Heather Mann and the relationship with Cecil soon petered out. The only real threat was businesswoman Amanda Staveley, who Prince Philip thought was the ideal choice to be the next duchess of York. He had always vehemently opposed Andrew's remarriage to Fergie. In 2004, Andrew proposed, but Staveley turned him down.

Despite these conquests, Andrew did not think his millionaire playboy lifestyle left him out of touch. He told the *Tatler*: 'I am a good deal more down-to-earth than people would expect of a member of the royal family. The ivory tower is not a syndrome from which I suffer.' He also insisted to the Ministry of Defence's house journal *Focus*: 'My life is a great deal more ordinary than perhaps is portrayed in the media.'

Normal for a playboy prince, perhaps. In the year before he left the navy, he was seen with his old friends Ghislaine Maxwell and Jeffrey Epstein and Victoria's Secret model Heidi Klum at a 'pimps and hookers' party in an upscale New York nightclub. He was seen near a prostitute and other seedy characters. He was then photographed beside a topless waitress at a Chinese New Year reception. The *Daily Mail* also reported that he had befriended a drug dealer at a party in Los Angeles.

However, a woman who met him at a party in St Tropez complained: 'He doesn't have much conversation other than himself.'

'He's everything people tell you,' another said. 'Boorish, interrupts you and laughs at his own jokes.' Not much has changed since his days in school.

Then in January 2001, he was photographed on board a luxury yacht off the Thai island of Phuket surrounded by a bevy of topless beauties. He made no excuses for his presence, saying: 'I was just reading my book. I wasn't really aware of what everyone else was doing.'

In Thailand Andrew had toured the red-light district of Patong with a police bodyguard in tow. In one go-go bar—bearing the motto 'good food, cold drinks, hot girls'—he danced with half-naked young women. A regular said: 'You certainly wouldn't get a member of the Thai royal family in a place like this. The area is very raunchy and many of the girls are prostitutes.'

Aides at the Palace were said to have been furious, given his role as Britain's roving trade envoy. 'Heaven help Britain's exporters,' said *The Sunday Times*.

Some doubts were even expressed in the Palace. Once courtier said: 'If he goes off to America to promote business... Will he be going off with Ghislaine Maxwell to a nightclub? The trouble with Andrew is that his private life will, willy-nilly, intrude into his public role.'

Who Pays the Piper?

Within months of his appointment as the special representative for British trade and investment, Andrew had attracted complaints. Too often, the Foreign Office's protocol department said, he refused to stick to the agreed itinerary and 'left a trail of glass in his wake'.

'Andrew's relations around the world are dicey,' commented one official at the weekly heads of department meeting, 'He's showing bad judgement about people. He's rude, lashes out to lay down the law, and it's so difficult to sell him.'

'You can call me 'Andy',' he told one British rear-admiral.

'And you can call me 'sir',' the admiral replied.

Diplomats had been warned by the Foreign Office not to include adverse comments in their dispatches. Anything unfavourable was conveyed by telephone.

But what does a princes do if not travel in style on the tax payers expense? The public learnt that 'Air-Miles Andy' refused to fly on commercial airlines after the government published a list of his destinations, which included a golf tournament, a football match, and social visits to beautiful girlfriends across the globe. Pampered with private jets, he remained rude and arrogant. Typical of his behaviour was overheard in an early-morning exchange in his £13 million ski chalet in Verbier. A young guest was making tea when Andrew suddenly appeared.

Following complaints from embassies in the Middle East and Latin America, senior officials met to discuss 'the Andrew problem'. The Queen needed to be told. She prevaricated and suggested that Prince Philip be consulted. He was annoyed and advised that Andrew be officially told to 'sharpen up his act or lose his job'.

In 2003, it was reported that Andrew spent £325,000 on flights. That included £2,939 on a helicopter he used to make a 120-mile round trip to Oxford, and RAF planes to fly him to St Andrews for two golfing jaunts.

He took trip to the US that took in the Masters golf tournament. In 2004, he was criticized for taking an RAF jet to Northern Ireland, where he played a round of golf before turning up to a royal garden party late. That year a trip to Bahrain coincided with the Formula One grand prix. The *Mail on Sunday* noted: 'If Prince Andrew does not swiftly learn the limits of public patience, he will endanger not just his own position, but that of the monarchy as a whole.'

In 2005, the National Audit Office investigated forty-one of his journeys, including a £3,000 bill for a helicopter to a business lunch in Oxford, when the train would have cost £97, and three trips to golfing events as part of his captaincy of the Royal and Ancient golf club of St Andrews at a cost of some £32,000. Once it cost £4,645 for him to take an RAF jet to the course in Fife so he could finish eighteen holes. Taxpayers forked out £681 to fly him thirty-five miles to baby products giant Johnson & Johnson in High Wycombe. And it was £3,600 for a RAF jet to take him to a military base ninety miles away in Somerset in June. The total to the taxpayer for his flight was £565,000.

'In terms of the return on investment to the UK,' Andrew said, 'I would suggest that £500,000 is cheap at the price.'

These were the words of a shrewd business investor.

Nor did he draw his horns in. On top of the £249,000 he was given by the Queen, *The Sunday Times* reported in July 2008 that for 'the Duke of York's public role… the last year received £436,000 to cover his expenses.'

That year, Prince Andrew travelled to the US in a private jet cost a whopping £100,000. Then a trip to China and the Far East cost taxpayers £30,000 for transport and accommodation. In January 2009, a visit to Switzerland cost £21,700 in hotel, travel and other overheads. In all his travels in 2009 cost the taxpayers £140,000. The following year he was severely chastised for using the Queen's helicopter on a 146-mile trip hopping around official engagements which were in the same area.

He flew from party to party. 'The helicopter is very often the most efficient way of packing in as many engagements as we can,' he said, 'as well as taking in some of the country's the finest golf courses.'

Perhaps an effort to economize, Andrew hired contractors to build a nine-hole golf course in the landscaped grounds of Windsor Lodge. Saving the taxpayer thousands, he could cut out the helicopter and walk out of his back door to play a round.

But the expense continued. On 8 March 2011, the *Daily Telegraph* reported: 'In 2010, the Prince spent £620,000 as a trade envoy, including

£154,000 on hotels, food and hospitality and £465,000 on travel.'

On a visit to Bahrain, the deputy head of the mission, Simon Wilson, said that Andrew was 'more commonly known among the British diplomatic community in the Gulf as HBH: His Buffoon Highness. This nickname stemmed from his childish obsession with doing exactly the opposite of what had been agreed in pre-visit meetings with his staff.'

Tatania Gfoeller, Washington's ambassador to Kyrgyzstan, recorded how, speaking at a business event, Andrew called the UK's Serious Fraud Office 'idiots' for investigating bribery claims around an arms deal in Saudi Arabia and accused *Guardian* journalists of 'poking their noses everywhere' for reporting it.

'The problem with Andrew,' a senior Buckingham Palace official said in 2001, 'is that his mouth engages before his brain does.' Is that really the problem?

His jaunts around the world allowed his to collect a wide circle of dubious friends, including one-time Libya dictator Colonel Gaddafi and his son Saif al-Islam who is wanted by the International Criminal Court for crimes against humanity. Then there's Sakher el-Materi, the son-in-law of the deposed Tunisian president Zine al-Abidine Ben Ali, who Andrew entertained at Buckingham Palace three months before the regime collapsed. He went into exile in the Seychelles and was sentenced to sixteen years after being tried *in absentia* for corruption.

A trip to see the president of Azerbaijan led to the headline 'The Duke and the Despot', while a skiing trip with convicted Libyan gun runner called Tarek Kaituni and led to 'Prince Takes Holiday With Gun Smuggler'. Andrew was also said to have accepted a £20,000 gold necklace for Beatrice. During the Libyan Civil War in February 2011, Andrew's questionable connections there led UK shadow justice minister Christ Bryant call into question he suitability to be trade envoy.

Andrew went goose-shooting with Nursultan Nazarbayev, the president of Kazakhstan and the longest serving non-royal leader in the world, in office from 1990 to 2019. No election was judged free and fair since the country gained its independence from the Soviet Union. Nazarbayev has been accused of human rights abuses by several international organizations. It was through Nazarbayev that Andrew met Timur Kulibayev, his son-in-law, the Kazakh oligarch who bought South York at an inflated price.

Certainly, Andrew thinks he is above the rules. In 2002 he told a police officer who pulled him over for speeding that he was in a hurry—to get to a golf tournament, as it turned out—and drove off before he could be given a ticket. Three years later there was a stand-off at Melbourne airport in Australia when he refused to subject himself to routine security screening before boarding a flight to New Zealand. 'Who does he think he is?' one member of the airport security team said. 'What a pompous prick.'

He caused a diplomatic incident when he publicly criticised George W Bush's White House for failing to listen more to the advice of the British government over the post-war strategy for Iraq. 'It is frankly embarrassing,' said the *Guardian* said, 'that Britain should be represented in any capacity by such a halfwit.'

In the last year of his trade role, he clocked up 77,000 air miles. The year after, 2012, it was 93,500. The next year taxpayers funded a trip to New York for a series of official engagements that coincided with his daughter Princess Eugenie moving to the city. The timing, the Palace insisted, was a coincidence.

Love and Marriage

In early July 2016, fashion PR Violet von Westenholz set up a blind date. She was the daughter of former Olympic skier Baron Piers von Westenholz, a long-standing friend of Prince Charles, and had known Harry for much of his life.

'It was not as if he could go onto a dating website in order to find the right person,' she said.

Violet had met Meghan Markle while working as a PR director for Ralph Lauren. They quickly became friends. The meeting with Harry took place in the Soho House on London's Dean Street, the West End townhouse where Meghan was staying on a trip to London. Harry had been at a service in Belgium commemorating the Battle of the Somme, returning to London on 1 July, while Meghan was scheduled to leave for Toronto on 5 July. Having not watched *Suits*, she was a mystery to him.

'I'd never, never even heard about her until this friend said "Meghan Markle",' Harry said. 'When I walked into that room and saw her and there she was sitting there, I was like "Okay, well I'm going to have to really up my game here—sit down and make sure I've got good chat."'

At their first meeting, they spent three hours together. She sipped on a martini, while he drank beer, ignoring the nibbles that had been left out for them. Asked later when he knew that Meghan was 'the one' Harry said: 'The very first time I met her.' As with Andrew when he met Fergie, it was as if a switch was flipped. No more party prince for them from that moment on. After years with lashings of royal fun, all of a sudden their desires ground to a halt before one person.

The next day Harry and Meghan met again at the Soho House, this time for dinner. Eager for some privacy, they entered via the staff entrance and were served by just one waiter the entire night. The second date was another resounding success. That night, she shared a post on her public Instagram account. It was a photo of a Love Hearts sweet with the inscription 'Kiss me' and the caption 'Love hearts in #London'.

After just two dates, the couple took a huge leap by going on holiday together that August. They could have gone anywhere, staying in a sumptuous hotel or a luxurious private villa. George Clooney even offered his holiday home on Lake Como. Instead, the lovebirds went to Botswana to camp out under the stars in the middle of nowhere.

'We were really by ourselves—it was crucial to me to make sure we had the chance to get to know each other,' Harry said. He spent four to six weeks in the wilderness every summer, finding that there, he could be 'more like myself than anywhere else in the world', whatever that means. This was his seventh holiday in Botswana, his fourth with a female companion.

In December, Harry and Meghan were seen picking out a Christmas tree in London's Battersea Park and shopping in the West End in mufti. They then rang in the New Year together in London before taking a vacation in Norway to see the Northern Lights.

They returned to London's Soho House for Valentine's Day before attending Tom Inskip's wedding in Montego Bay. In May, they were photographed kissing for the first time after a polo match in Ascot. The following month, *Daily Mail* reported that Harry gave Meghan a gold thumb ring. The jewellery joined a collection of other gifts—a blue and white bracelet, which matched his own, a Cartier Love bracelet, a Maya Brenner necklace with 'M' and 'H' initials and a gold arrow ring.

They returned to Botswana in August for Meghan's thirty-sixth birthday. This time they spent three weeks at Meno a Kwena, a $1,000-a-night safari lodge. On their return to England, Harry arranged a secret meeting for Meghan with the Queen. The couple then flew to Scotland to visit Charles and Camilla at Balmoral.

In September, Meghan made her first public appearance alongside the prince at the Invictus Games in Toronto. She graced the cover of the October issue of *Vanity Fair* over the cover line: 'She's Just Wild About Harry.'

Harry and Meghan also spent time together in Nottingham Cottage. It was smaller than Meghan's home in Canada. One Sunday evening, they were having a night-in at Nottingham Cottage when Harry went down on one knee and proposed. Her answer was an instant yes.

Like Andrew, Harry had designed the ring himself. Made by court jewellers, Cleave and Company, it was made of yellow gold and carried one diamond from Botswana and two smaller diamonds from Princess Diana's collection.

Harry said that if Diana had been alive today, she and Meghan would be as 'thick as thieves'. Eighteen months later, Meghan replaced the yellow gold band with one that was studded with diamonds.

William and Kate had warned Harry against rushing into a relationship with Meghan and reports surfaced that Harry did not have his older brother's blessing to go public about it. The couple commissioned New York-based fashion photographer Alexi Lubomirski to take the engagement photos at Frogmore Cottage in Windsor. Meghan's sheer Ralph & Russo ball gown caused some serious controversy with some claiming the nude top wasn't appropriate for the soon-to-be royal.

Meghan spent her first Christmas with Harry, the Queen, and the rest of the royal family at Sandringham in 2017. 'The family loved having her there,' Harry said afterwards. In March, the Queen wrote to the Privy Council, declaring officially her consent to the marriage.

The wedding took place in St. George's Chapel in Windsor on 19 May 2018. British and foreign royalty turned out, along with the regular celebs and the cast of *Suits*. It was estimated to have cost £32 million.

On the morning of his wedding, the Queen made Harry the Duke of Sussex and Meghan the Duchess. He was also given the Scottish title Earl of Dumbarton and the Irish title Baron Kilkeel. Two months later he was promoted to the rank of major, while also being made a lieutenant commander in the Royal Navy and a squadron leader in the RAF despite not having served in those services. In the royal family you need all the ranks you can get.

He became patron of Walk America, a thousand-mile trek across the United States undertaken by veterans. While not joining in the trek itself, he was 'embarking on his own special relationship,' the US ambassador to Britain said. *Time* magazine named him as one of the 100 Most Influential People in the World, though it was not clear on what grounds.

The couple delayed their honeymoon to attend a garden party at Buckingham Palace celebrating Charles' seventieth birthday.

In October, they made an official visit to Australia, New Zealand and Tonga, attending the Invictus Games that was held in Sydney that year, a week after they announced that Meghan was going to have a baby in the spring. She flew to New York on a private jet for a $500,000 baby shower that was held in the penthouse of the Mark Hotel. At $75,000-a-night it is said to be the most expensive hotel room in America.

The jet was said to have cost £100,000, prompting environmentalists to question her green credentials. She faced accusations of 'hypocrisy' over the couple's campaigns to tackle poverty and climate change.

During the last leg of their Australian tour the previous October, Harry had called for action to save the planet. A spokesman for Friends of the Earth told *Mail Online*: 'Private air travel obviously comes with a huge carbon footprint. Perhaps for future trips the Duchess could consider less carbon intensive modes of travel. We invite her to set a good climate trend by flying less.'

One Twitter user said: 'Meghan & Harry are being billed as Humanitarians. They are Patrons of charities for the disadvantaged. The obscene cost of this 5-day trip is utter hypocrisy. Not to mention the carbon footprint of taking a private jet.'

Another added: 'Meghan proving she's no Duchess. The obscene expense of the trip coupled with the utter hypocrisy of private jets by someone who claims they care for the environment...'

Despite this, after returning from Australia, the couple seized the chance to take a quick holiday in Morocco.

Meghan was heavily pregnant when they moved into Frogmore Cottage, in the grounds adjoining Windsor Castle, in April 2019. The cottage was five-bedroom property. A gift from the Queen, it was said it required 'a substantial overhaul'. The refurbishment has cost UK taxpayers £2.4 million pounds and sparked public fury. It was the beginning of the souring between the Sussexes and the British public.

Having left Kensington Palace, they set up their own Instagram account @SussexRoyal, leaving the official Kensington Palace account to William and Kate. The Sussex's first post was their official monogram which blends the first letters of Harry and Meghan's names into a single icon, topped with a coronet and 'Official Instagram for their Royal Highnesses the Duke and Duchess of Sussex' written beneath it.

Their first child Archie Harrison Mountbatten-Windsor was born at the Portland Hospital in London on 6 May 2019 and was then sixth in line to the throne. He was christened wearing the royal christening gown by the Archbishop of Canterbury on 6 July 2019 in the private chapel at Windsor Castle, with water from the River Jordan.

Showing their continued dedication to Africa, Harry and Meghan took a ten-day trip with Archie, who they introduced to Desmond Tutu. However, the couple's relationship with the press and the rest of the royal family was beginning to sour.

Just Weird, Right?

Throughout his time of rubbing shoulders with the rich and famous—and, in some cases, corrupt—Andrew had got to know Jeffery Epstein. After his link to the convicted paedophile became public with the photograph of the two of them strolling in Central Park was published in the *News of the World* in August 2011, Andrew stepped down as trade envoy to dedicate himself to his playboy career fulltime. In 2010, he was photographed on a 154-foot yacht off the coast of Sardinia with a half-Spanish, half-Filipino model Alexandra Escat, who was half the Prince's age.

She later recounted how she fetched Andrew some sunscreen and was taken aback when he asked her to apply it for him. 'This is somebody I have barely met and he's royal. I mean, that's just weird, right?'

Just a week after the photo of Andrew and Epstein, which had been taken in December 2010, appeared in the papers, Andrew's press secretary, Ed Perkins, got a phone call from Sian James, an assistant editor at the *Mail on Sunday*, who told him that they had obtained and interview with Virginia Roberts. She claimed that Epstein had turned her into an underage prostitute and had taken her to London, at age seventeen, to have sex with Prince Andrew. It couldn't be published. Andrew unequivocally denied the story from the moment the claim was made.

But the paper did have a picture of Andrew with his arm around Giuffre's bare midriff which it published alongside a different story of a 21-one-year old woman who said she sat on the prince's lap. Also in the picture was Ghislaine Maxwell who Roberts was to accuse in 2015 of recruiting her as Epstein's sex slave. Roberts said the picture had been taken by Epstein. The photograph (both the back and front) were copied at her by a respected *Mail on Sunday* photographer

It was awkward enough. Andrew was embroiled in another scandal at the time. The cash-strapped Fergie had been caught offering access to Andrew for £500,000 by an undercover reporter for the *News of the World* posing as a businessman. The meeting had been secretly filmed.

'If you want to meet him in your business, look after me, and he'll look after you. You'll get it back tenfold,' Fergie could be heard saying on the video. 'That opens up everything you would ever wish for. And I can open any door you want. And I will for you.'

Chris Bryant, who was a Foreign Office minister at the time Andrew held his trade envoy role, demanded a parliamentary inquiry into the prince's business behaviour. 'It all just stinks,' said Bryant. 'I don't think he has ever been able to draw a distinction between his own personal interest and the national interest. It's morally offensive. He clearly was never fit to hold that office.'

Although Andrew was not Britain's trade envoy anymore, other public duties continued. In 2013, he was elected a royal fellow of the Royal Society, but Britain's pre-eminent scientific institution faced unprecedented dissent from members over the move, with one professor describing the duke as an 'unsavoury character'. He had no background in science.

Car Crash

During much of the time Andrew was jaunting around the world as the UK's trade envoy, he was also stopping off to see Epstein and stay at his various homes. But then, apart from the meeting in December 2010 and watching The King's Speech with him, Andrew had broken off contact with the billionaire following his conviction for sexual offences in 2008. However, this did not leave Andrew in the clear. He had already been named in legal documents.

In 2011, the embarrassing headlines the allegations spawned and their impact on the prince's taxpayer-funded role as UK trade envoy were discussed at the highest levels of government in 10 Downing Street. Legal paperwork, held by lawyers in West Palm Beach acting for some of the fourteen girls who have lodged suits against fifty-eight-year-old Epstein, also named Prince Andrew's friend Ghislaine Maxwell, Epstein's girlfriend, as an abuser

Epstein had been under investigation for having sex with underage girls since 2005. The following year the FBI stepped in, but Epstein's lawyer Harvard law professor Alan Dershowitz cut a 'sweet-heart deal' whereby Epstein pled guilty to two state felony prostitution charges and was sentenced to eighteen months, plus paying restitution to over thirty other victims identified by the FBI. Instead of going to state prison, he was given a private wing of the Palm Beach County Sheriff's Stockade, paying $128,000 to the Police Department for the privilege. After just three months, he was granted work release that allowed him out of jail for up to sixteen hours, seven days a week at an office at the Florida Science Foundation, an organization he had set up. After thirteen months he was released, ostensibly on probation.

To celebrate the completion of his sentence, Epstein held a dinner party at his New York town house where the guest of honour was Prince Andrew. Andrew stayed for four days, and it was during that trip he was photograph strolling the Central Park with Epstein.

However, the accusations against Epstein would not go away. Victims sued the Federal Government for making a settlement with Epstein without informing them and Julia K. Brown of the *Miami Herald* went to work and identified some eighty victims. Lo and behold, the name of Prince Andrew kept on coming up. He had been frequent guest of Epstein's and had attended parties, it was alleged.

Waiving her rights of anonymity Virginia Roberts spoke out in her court case against Maxwell. She said that she had been recruited by Maxwell from Donald Trump's Mar-a-Lago club. She had been used as a sex slave by Maxwell and Epstein and trafficked to other influential men. At seventeen, she had allegedly been flown to London at Epstein's expense to have sex with Prince Andrew. The accusation was firmly denied by him.

On 6 July 2019, federal agents were waiting on the tarmac when his private jet, the Lolita Express, landed at Teterboro airport in New Jersey. Epstein was arrested and charged with sex trafficking and conspiracy to traffic minors for sex. On August 10th, Epstein died under suspicious circumstances in his cell while awaiting trial at the Metropolitan Correctional Center. Ghislaine Maxwell went on the run.

No doubt, with the death of Epstein, many of the big names associated with him—including Donald Trump and Bill Clinton—breathed a sigh of relief. Apart from accusing each other of Epstein's murder, they kept out of the limelight. Prince Andrew thought he knew better.

At the behest of Fergie and his daughter Princess Beatrice, Andrew sought to 'clear his name' before Giuffre could give an interview—or, at least, draw a line under his association with Epstein. The BBC's *Newsnight* could not believe their luck when he agreed to an hour-long interview. He even agreed to do it in a state room in Buckingham Palace, his mother's office, to assert his authority.

Under only gentle prodding by interviewer Emily Maitlis, Andrew said he could not recall ever meeting Virginia Roberts. He could not have been in Tramp with her as he had been in the Pizza Express in Woking with Beatrice that evening. Nor could he have bought her a drink as he did not even know where the bar was in Tramp.

Virginia also remembered that he had sweated profusely on the dance floor.

'There's a slight problem with the sweating because I have a peculiar medical condition which is that I don't sweat or I didn't sweat at the time,' he said. 'I didn't sweat at the time because I had suffered what I would describe as an overdose of adrenalin in the Falkland's War when I was shot at and I simply... it was almost impossible for me to sweat.'

Nor could he explain the photograph of him with his arm around her waist with Ghislaine Maxwell in her Belgravia home. Friends of his had suggested it was fake, though experts can find no evidence of that and the photographer of the pictures confirmed he had seen the original in 2011.

He had only gone to stay with Epstein after his conviction to break off the relationship as 'it was inappropriate for us to be seen together' in future. Before that, he had known nothing of Epstein's wrongdoing. He conceded that the visit was 'not the wisest thing to do', but 'I had to show leadership'. Besides, his town house, where many of Epstein's crimes were said to have taken place, was 'a convenient place to stay'. He noticed nothing awry though others who visited had.

'My judgement,' he reckoned, 'was probably coloured by my tendency to be too honourable.'

Nor did he regret his friendship with Epstein—'the reason being is that the people that I met and the opportunities that I was given to learn either by him or because of him were actually very useful.'

He also conceded that his conduct had been 'unbecoming'. But he did not take the opportunity to express any sympathy for Epstein's victims. He would later do so when settling the Giuffre lawset and include a promise to make a contribution to her victims' charity.

While the viewing public were aghast, Andrew thought the interview had been a triumph. He even told the Queen so. The press did not agree and thought it was a farce. Channel 4 commissioned a musical on the prince, and film companies swept up the rights for not one but two participants' biopics in the prince's epic debacle. Andrew was forced to stand down from public life and hide behind the walls of Royal Lodge in Windsor Great Park up to and after the coronation of King Charles III to stay personally out of the public eye. The palace, however, allowed him to appear in the wild for ecclesiastical ceremonies, such as the funeral of the Queen, Christmas and Easter, in a pack of other royals.

Andrew's performance appeared even more ludicrous when the BBC had another bite at the cherry. Two weeks after Andrew's interview aired, *Panorama* broadcast an interview with Virginia Giuffre. She dismissed his denials and 'ridiculous excuses' such as that the photograph of them together might have been doctored.

'I mean I'm calling BS on this, because that's what it is,' she said. 'He knows what happened. I know what happened. And there's only one of us telling the truth.'

A Federal judge in a civil case seemed to give her the benefit of the doubt. In August 2021, she sued Andrew for 'sexual assault and intentional infliction of emotional distress'. When her lawyers tried to serve the legal papers on him, he fled to Scotland to hide behind mummy's skirt at Balmoral. After Virginia's legal team threatened to get the High Court in London to serve the papers, the gate keeper at the Royal Lodge eventually accepted them. Rather than man up and go to the US to clear his name, he settled out of court for an undisclosed sum of money reported to be as much as £12 million.

Two years later, a campaign started to get the settlement which he had voluntarily entered. As part of this, Ghislaine Maxwell's brother Ian volunteered a photograph of two friends in the bath at her Belgrave home with pictures of Andrew and Virginia over their faces. This was supposed to show that Andrew could not have had sex in the bath with Virginia as she had alleged. The picture—which appeared on the front page of the *Daily Telegraph*—raised the scandal to new heights of farce. Putting two people in a bath could hardly prove that two people could not fit in a bath. What's more, it showed that it was a big enough bath. There was room for Ghislaine, who was five foot five like Giuffre, to join them if she had been so inclined.

Meanwhile, Ghislaine had been tracked down by the FBI, who claimed that they had known where she was all the time. She had given journalists the run-around.—Ghislaine was apprehended at the aptly named 'Tuckedaway', a discreet mansion in Bradford, New Hampshire, less than 150 miles from the Canadian border.

Charged with sex trafficking, she was held in the Metropolitan Detention Center in Brooklyn for 18 months. Her lawyers argued that she should be bailed so she could move to the Waldorf-Astoria. At her trial, her defence team sought to discredit her accusers by alleging they were gold-diggers, though Maxwell herself had made tens of millions out of pandering for Epstein. But she did not take the stand in her own defence and was sentenced to twenty years.

Prince Andrew did not appear as a character witness in her defence—not that it would have helped in all likelihood given the headlines. When the FBI sought his help in the case, he ignored their requested. The US Department of Justice then made a formal requests to the British Home Office under the Mutual Legal Assistance Treaty. Under that Treaty, if he did not co-operate, he was to answer in a British court. He has not done so as far as we know today. It means that technically he may be a fugitive from US justice.

From behind bars in the Federal Correctional Institution in Tallahassee, Florida, Maxwell gave a statement supporting her 'dear friend' Prince Andrew. But Andrew has denied that she is a good friend even though they have known each other for over forty years and been photographed together on numerous occasions, not least in Maxwell's Belgrave house with Virginia Roberts.

National Treasures

While Andrew had been unceremoniously kicked out of the Firm by his mother, stripped of his royal patronages, honorary military titles and any official use of his HRH title, Harry quit voluntarily, even at one point threatening to drop the Sussex title before the royal family could change their minds.

At first, he and Meghan tried to slip away quietly. On the 8th of January, 2020, they revealed that they would be stepping down as working. They felt they were being driven out after being told they would not have major roles in the slimmed-down monarchy William and Charles were planning, a friend has claimed. *The Times* reported that they regarded themselves as having been pushed away by what they saw as a bullying attitude from the Duke of Cambridge. Others blamed Meghan, who the *Daily Mail* said was on the brink of meltdown before the announcement was made. Harry may have dropped the news early, partly out of concern for Meghan's mental and emotional health, the newspaper said.

The couple shared that they intended to work to become 'financially independent'. This would not be a struggle. Harry had inherited £10 million from his mother and another £6 million from this great-grandmother, Queen Elizabeth the Queen Mother. What he subsequently inherited from Prince Philip (a penniless immigrant made good) and the Queen (reportedly the richest woman in the world) has not been disclosed. He had also been receiving £2.3 million a year from his father and may have put some aside for a rainy day. The *Daily Telegraph* estimated that he was worth £30 million. Meghan was hardly a pauper either. For the seven years she worked on *Suits*, she was reportedly paid $50,000 an episode, or $450,000 a year.

Harry and Meghan said that they would be splitting their time in the future between the United Kingdom and North America. 'This geographic balance will enable us to raise our son with an appreciation for the royal tradition into which he was born, while also providing our family with the space to focus on the next chapter, including the launch of our new charitable entity,' they wrote.

It was reported that they had not even informed the Queen of their decision before making the announcement. Meghan fled back to Canada leaving Harry to handle a conference call from his grandmother, father, and older brother. The *Sun* dubbed her departure 'Megxit'. #Megxit was soon trending on Twitter.

The British tabloids were hostile. This was hardly surprising as Meghan was suing Associated Newspapers, the parent company of the *Mail on Sunday*, and the newspaper itself after it published a private letter from Meghan to her father. In a short statement, which apparently had not been cleared by the Palace, Harry said that Meghan had 'become one of the latest victims of a British tabloid press that wages campaigns against individuals with no thought to the consequences'. He complained of the 'relentless propaganda' against her. Earlier, he had drawn attention to the 'racial undertones of comment pieces and the outright sexism and racism of social media trolls and web article comments'.

True, *MailOnline* had run a headline saying Meghan was '(Almost) Straight Outta Compton'. Harry pointed out that she had never lived in Compton or anywhere near it.

The American media joined in attributing Megxit to racism. While admitting that Meghan had suffered racist remarks on internet platforms, the *Daily Telegraph's* claim that the British press was institutionally racist was absurd. Middle England had fawned over the couple when they got engaged and faithful monarchist had toasted their wedding at street parties, while the press had hailed Meghan as a 'breath of fresh air'. Her mixed heritage was initially seen as an advantage especially in the couple's dealings with the Commonwealth.

But it wasn't long before the whiff of rot set in, the newspaper said, citing the secrecy over Archie's christening which did not sit comfortably alongside revelations about the £2.4 million refurbishment of Frogmore Cottage paid for by the taxpayer. Nor did heckling the public on climate change while zipping around on private jets go down well.

'Britain's frustration with the Sussexes thus centres around their hypocrisy and self-destructive determination to have their cake and eat it,' wrote columnist Sherelle Jacobs. 'Yes, there is a disconnect between the royal pair and swathes of Britain. Not because Meghan has foreign ancestors, but due to the fact that the couple seem to live on another PR-oiled, celebno-cratic planet. As reflected in their new website which toothily techno-jabbers about going forward in a 'progressive new role' and continuing to 'collaborate' with Her Majesty.'

Harry continued to insist that there was 'no other option' but to stand down so that he could be with the woman he loved. Soon he joined her in Canada, while Netflix began making overtures. Ten days after the Sussexes' resignation tweet, the Queen issued a statement saying: 'Following many months of conversations and more recent discussions, I am pleased that together we have found a constructive and supportive way forward for my grandson and his family. Harry, Meghan, and Archie will always be much loved members of my family.'

She added that she was 'particularly proud of how Meghan has so quickly become one of the family'.

A statement from Buckingham Palace said: 'The Duke and Duchess of Sussex are grateful to Her Majesty and the Royal Family for their ongoing support as they embark on the next chapter of their lives.'

Under the new arrangement, Harry and Meghan understood that they were required to step back from royal duties, including official military appointments—Harry had inherited the role of Captain General of the Royal Marines from Prince Philip. The couple would no longer receive public funds for royal duties. However, they were allowed to continue their private interests.

'With The Queen's blessing, the Sussexes will continue to maintain their private patronages and associations. While they can no longer formally represent The Queen, the Sussexes have made clear that everything they do will continue to uphold the values of Her Majesty.'

They would no longer use their HRH titles and would pay back the money spent on refurbishing Frogmore Cottage, which would remain their family home in the UK. In future, they would pay a 'commercial rent', though it was not clear how that would be assessed. Your average estate agent would not know how to price a Grade II listed building in a royal park. In any case, the couple intended to spend most of their time in North America. Prince Charles would also continue to provide financial support he said, though Harry complained later that he had been cut off without a penny.

The Palace statement did not address who was going to pay for the Sussexes' security in future. The Canadian government made it clear that they did not want to pick up the tab and would provide no security for the couple after 31 March 2021. They had been paying the bill since November 2019.

By late March, the couple had moved to the US where President Donald Trump also said the government would not pay for the Sussexes' security. They moved into secure housing in Beverley Hills provided by Tyler Perry, said to be the highest-paid man in entertainment. In July, they bought a mansion in Montecito, California. The American private security firm, Gavin de Becker and Associates, was contracted to provide security, though the Santa Barbara County Sheriff's Office were called nine times in as many months when alarms were activated.

The couple were forced to drop the Sussex Royal brand name, with the Sussex royal website and Instagram account being closed down as the couple had agreed to stop using the term 'royal' for commercial or charitable activities. Their offices in Buckingham Palace were also closed and the US PR consultants Sunshine Sachs took over the handling of their image. The company's other clients have included Barbara Streisand, Ben Affleck, Justin Timberlake, the Michael Jackson estate, and Harvey Weinstein—who, of course, was in Ghislaine's little black book and had been invited, along with Epstein, to Windsor Castle to Andrew's daughter Princess Beatrice's eighteenth birthday in July 2006, two months after an arrest warrant had been issued for Epstein for the sexual assault of minor. It was also announced that the couple would no longer co-operate with the British tabloids.

The Sussexes' new chief of staff Catherine St Laurant, formerly an employee of the Bill & Melinda Gates Foundation, would run their non-profit organization. They also set up the Archewell Foundation which called itself 'an impact-driven non-profit' whose 'core purpose is to uplift and unite communities—local and global, online and offline—one act of compassion at a time'. It signed multi-million-dollar deals with Spotify and Netflix.

Just two months after Harry and Meghan stepped down, the book *Finding Freedom: Harry, Meghan and the Making of a Modern Royal Family*, a biography of the Duke and Duchess authored by royal reporters Carolyn Durand and Omid Scobie, was published. While the Sussexes' denied lending any assistance to the authors, *The Spectator* wrote: 'Despite revealing details that presumably only people who were in the room when it happened could ever conceivably know, we are expected to believe that Carolyn Durand and Omid Scobie wrote *Finding Freedom* without input from the Sussexes.' The book reproduced word-for-word Prince William's advice to Harry on marrying Meghan.

It was hard not to conclude that Harry had taken a leaf out of his mother's book when she co-operated with Andrew Morton on *Diana: Her True Story* that rocked her relationship with the royal family in 1992. Meghan's legal team later admitted she had permitted a close friend to communicate with Durand and Scobie 'to set the record straight'. The book topped the bestseller lists on both sides of the Atlantic.

After Morton's book, Diana went on to tell her story on TV in an interview with Martin Bashir. Charles had followed suit with an TV interview and authorised with Jonathan Dimbleby. This did not work out well for either party. Andrew's TV car crash came next.

Harry failed to heed to the warning signs. He and Meghan went on TV with Oprah Winfrey in a programme that netted somewhere between $7 million and $9 million, according to the *Wall Street Journal*. They must have been short on money. Andrew must have been kicking himself. The BBC had not even paid expenses.

If the couple's relations with the rest of the royal family were not bad enough, Harry talked of his estrangement from his father and brother, while Meghan said that an unidentified member of the royal family had asked what 'how dark' their unborn child would come out.

Asked if there were concerns Archie might be 'too brown', Meghan told Oprah that was a pretty safe assumption. Both she and Harry refused to identify the person, saying it would be very damaging. Strangely though, for regular families, both black and white, this would be considered a perfectly natural question. But, on Oprah, this was implied racism—or unconscious bias as the freshly woke Harry would term it.

Curiously, while the couple sought to distance themselves from the royal family, Meghan complained that Archie was being denied the title of prince, unlike Prince William's son Prince George, suggesting it was due to Archie being mixed-race. Further damaging the mystique, Meghan announced that the royal wedding, watched by some thirty million viewers across the world, had been a sham. The couple had been married secretly in a private ceremony three days earlier. The Archbishop of Canterbury said this was not true. It had merely been a rehearsal.

The confines of palace life affected her mental health Meghan said, telling Winfrey that her driving license, passport, and credit cards had been taken from her, leaving her a virtual prisoner—though she was carefree enough to fly the Atlantic for a baby shower. Harry said he believed that, after he and Meghan toured Australia in October 2018, members of the royal family were jealous of the effortless manner that Meghan had been able to interact with people in the Commonwealth and 'how good she was at the job'. Again, this echoed Diana who had stolen the limelight. Nearly fifty million viewers watched the interview worldwide.

Dumb and Dumber

The Palace panicked and there was a crisis meeting of senior royals. Meanwhile Harry's popularity plunged. In Britain, a YouGov poll showed that 48 per cent of respondents now had a negative view of Harry, compared with 45 per cent with a positive view. This was the first time his net favourability rating had been negative, and a fall of 15 points from the previous week.

Nevertheless, Harry continued his veiled criticism of the royal family, telling *Armchair Expert* podcast host Dax Shepard: 'If I've experienced some form of pain or suffering because of the pain or suffering that perhaps my father or my parents had suffered, I'm going to make sure I break that cycle so that I don't pass it on.'

He particularly had his father in his sights.

'I started to piece it together and go: 'Okay, so this is where he went to school, this is what happened, I know this about his life, I also know that is connected to his parents so that means he's treated me the way he was treated, so how can I change that for my own kids?" Harry said.

He regularly complained about the media intrusion into his life, yet he was happy to share pictures and video of his own children. Indeed, judging by the footage they've share, the Sussexes rarely go anywhere without a camera crew.

Harry compared his life to a mixture of the film *The Truman Show*, where the main character unwittingly lives his life in a reality TV show. One can see Jim Carrey as Harry and Harry playing a pet detective or, with his Uncle Andrew, playing *Dumb and Dumber*.

Being born into the royal family, Harry said, 'you inherit every element of it without choice', including that the UK media 'feel an ownership over you'.

In his early twenties, he had thought: 'I don't want this job, I don't want to be here. I don't want to be doing this. Look what it did to my mum. How am I ever going to settle down and have a wife and family when I know that it's going to happen again? I've seen behind the curtain, I've seen the business model. I know how this operation runs and how it works, I don't want to be part of this.'

After a conversation with Meghan, he said he decided to go to therapy.

'Suddenly it was like the bubble was burst,' he said. 'I plucked my head out of the sand, gave it a good shake off and I was like: 'Okay, you're in this position of privilege, stop complaining or stop thinking as though you want something different. Make this different, because you can't get out.''

This precipitated their move to California.

'Living here now I can actually lift my head and I feel different, my shoulders have dropped, so have hers. You can walk around feeling a little bit more free. I can take Archie on the back of my bicycle. I would never have had the chance to do that.'

Harry was seeking a new role; it was announced that he had become the first chief impact officer of BetterUp Inc, a San Francisco-based start-up that provides employee coaching and mental health assistance. He had already been making a series of documentaries about mental health with Oprah Winfrey for Apple TV+.

Harry went on to alienate the American media by saying the First Amendment to the US Constitution guaranteeing free speech was 'bonkers'. Previously the Sussexes had restricted their criticism of the media to the British tabloid press and the BBC.

Republican Texas congressman Dan Crenshaw claimed that this remark had 'just doubled the size of my Independence Day party'. Fox News' Laura Ingraham added: 'Don't let the doorknob hit you, Windsor.' She continued: 'It's supposed to be a life of service, right?... But I think he seems to have gotten off track. I feel bad, feel bad for him, but you can't be piling on your family every five seconds.'

Then there was a swipe at his Apple TV documentary *The Me You Can't See*: 'What else are they going to do? They have got to come up with original content. They're making all this money, right. This is all they have.'

Nigel Farage pitched in: 'For Prince Harry to condemn the USA's First Amendment shows he has lost the plot. Soon he will not be wanted on either side of the pond.'

Harry and Meghan's daughter was born on 4 June 2021 in Santa Barbara Cottage Hospital. They named her Lilibet Diana. Unlike her father, she did have a surname: Mountbatten-Windsor. Prince Philip had instituted just before Andrew's birth that any royal child born to one of his children who was without a title would get his surname and the Windsor one. It was the name 'Lilibet' that immediately courted controversy as the Queen was nicknamed Lilibet in the family when she was a toddler. The BBC reported that they had not asked the Queen's permission. This was denied by the Sussexes and the Palace, but its play in the media did little to heal the rift.

Things could only get worse when it was reported that Harry was being given an advance of $20 million for an explosive memoir. In press release from his publisher Penguin Random House, he said: 'I'm writing this not as the prince I was born but as the man I have become. I've worn many hats over the years, both literally and figuratively, and my hope is that in telling my story—the highs and lows, the mistakes, the lessons learned—I can help show that no matter where we come from, we have more in common than we think.

'I'm deeply grateful for the opportunity to share what I've learned over the course of my life so far and excited for people to read a first-hand account of my life that's accurate and wholly truthful.'

It could only get worse. While the Platinum Jubilee put the Queen back centre stage, the death of Prince Philip and then the Queen was overshadowed by arguments about what uniforms Andrew and Harry were going to be allowed to wear.

Then came six hours of Harry and Meghan whinging on Netflix. Coincidentally Virginia Giuffre appeared on Netflix's *Filthy Rich*. Then came the icing on the cake—Harry's autobiography *Spare*. 'My Story, My Words,' said *People* magazine. But it was no secret that it was the work of a ghost writer.

And it told you everything you didn't want to know—losing his virginity to an older woman in a field behind a pub, frostbite on his 'todger' and the glutinous description of his romance with Meghan which would have proved too saccharin for the editors at Mills & Boon. The reader is spared no intimate detail. Then, for a man worried about his security, there's the admission that he killed twenty-five Taliban, which put him right back as number one on the terrorist hit list. And the US immigration authorities might have something to say about his admission of the repeated use of illegal drugs.

All this guaranteed a collapse in the polls. After publication, Harry had just 10 per cent support in UK polls, with 53 per cent holding negative opinion. Meghan, who had gone to ground, had a 19 per cent approval rating with 55 per cent against. Only Andrew was more unpopular. In the US, Harry plunged from +38 to -7 while Meghan fell from +23 to -13.

Even still, Harry has more to say. He reckons that he has enough material for a second volume of his autobiography. Is he aiming to become the most unpopular royal since Ivan the Terrible or Ming the Merciless? Or is it a battle to the bottom with Uncle Andrew, who seems to cultivate the delusion that he can recapture in the hearts and minds of the British people. Meanwhile the gagging order on Virginia Giuffre imposed by her settlement with Andrew—presumably to keep her quiet during the Jubilee—is about to be lifted. She shows no sign of wanting to say silent. Indeed, there is talk of a tell-all autobiography.

The royal family are an expensive team to keep on as Britain's top representatives. They are also usually not the sharpest pencils (apologies King Charles, pens). But there is one thing you can't fault them on. Their public squabbling over royal names titles and property, as well as attempts to make money either off the state or the public, offer entertainment value to their subjects if not the rest of the world and a helpful guide on what not to do.

Andrew's job as spare consisted of forever pleasing the monarch despite being becoming a perpetual drag on the Firm due to his unfailing ability to do the wrong thing. When he at last found a successful vehicle—Pitch at the Palace, a global organisation involved with tech start-ups—to frame his life with, he shot his own organisation in the foot by giving a BBC interview on his friendship with and 3-day visit in 2010 to convicted sex-pervert Jeffrey Epstein. He hasn't shown himself in public except when cordoned off by a donut of royal relatives and his job has come to end. Nothing will please Charles III except Andrew's disappearance from the royal front line.

Will Andrew take this lying down? Unlikely. His self belief is infinite and so he feels deeply wronged by the adverse responses to his own *faux pas*. Like Monty Python's Black Knight, he will say till the last, 'Come back here and take what's coming to you!' But in the same way that the court supported Andrew up till 2022, the palace will ineluctably grind away all privileges. After cresting for sixty years, the influence of the House of York has passed.

It is Harry who has finally come in to his own. He 'didn't know how to be' he complained in *Spare*. He's finally found a direction for all his aggression and is aiming it straight at the family who made him feel a nullity. Diana, of course, did the same thing during the period she was upset with the royal family. He has certainly now found a release for his 'red mist'. He may not be an afficionado of his family's history, but there are plenty of examples of princes raining discontent on the monarch from abroad. Like the popes in Avignon, he is fashioning a role as the anti-Heir: no jacket and tie or other formality for him, lots of talk of earthy subjects to show that at heart he is happy to use the media as his platform. As Andrew's star is in terminal decline, Harry is in the ascendant and will remain a thorn in the side of the monarchy for as long as his Charles III reigns.

As with Andrew, it would have taken just a small effort to nip Harry's going rogue in the bud early on. But the world of royalty from matters more than substance. Harry recalls sleeping in Balmoral where the 'bedding was clean, crisp, various shades of white', much of it stamped with ER, Elizabeth Regina, all if pulled tight like piano wire so that the patched holes and tears of the past century were clearly visible. Buckingham Palace would rather have Harry than ever having to admit it was wrong.

Printed in the USA
CPSIA information can be obtained
at www.ICGtesting.com
JSHW031002030424
60434JS00008B/70

9 781783 342488